UNSHAKEABLE

UNSHAKEABLE

JOHN ECKHARDT

CHARISMA
HOUSE

UNSHAKEABLE by John Eckhardt
Published by Charisma House
Charisma Media/Charisma House Book Group
600 Rinehart Road
Lake Mary, Florida 32746
www.charismahouse.com

Cover design by Justin Evans

Visit the author's website at www.johneckhardt.global.

Library of Congress Cataloging-in-Publication Data:
Eckhardt, John, 1957
  Unshakeable / by John Eckhardt.
    pages cm
  Includes bibliographical references.

ISBN 978-1-62998-594-7 (trade paper) -- ISBN 978-1-62998-595-4
(e-book)
  1. Spiritual warfare. 2. Thought and thinking--Religious aspects--
Christianity. I. Title.
  BV4509.5.E347 2015
  248.4--dc23

2015021973

Portions of this book were previously published by Charisma House
as *Deliverance and Spiritual Warfare Manual*, ISBN 978-1-62136-
625-6, copyright © 2014 and *God's Covenant for Deliverance and
Freedom*, ISBN 978-1-62136-579-2, copyright © 2014.

20 21 22 23 24 — 10 9 8 7 6
Printed in the United States of America

CONTENTS

CHAPTER 1

SATAN'S MASTER PLAN TO DESTROY THE HUMAN RACE

This Is Double-Mindedness

The thief does not come, except to steal and kill and destroy.

—JOHN 10:10

I N 1886 SCOTTISH author Robert Louis Stevenson wrote the best-selling novella *The Strange Case of Dr. Jekyll and Mr. Hyde.* The story is about the abnormal behavior Gabriel John

Utterson, a London lawyer, observes in his old friend Dr. Henry Jekyll and Jekyll's alter ego, Edward Hyde. According to one source, "The work is commonly associated with the rare mental condition often spuriously called 'split personality,' wherein within the same person there are at least two distinct personalities. In this case, the two personalities in Dr. Jekyll are apparently good and evil, with completely opposite levels of morality."[1] This story has had such an impact on our culture and language, that when we see people act one way one minute and switch to something completely different, we sometimes say they are like "Jekyll and Hyde."

What Stevenson wrote was fiction, but it amplifies the problem of a dual personality. It has even become a part of the language. Of course most people don't come to the level of psychosomatic dysfunction as Jekyll-Hyde, but life often imitates art in some way. In this case, the spirit of double-mindedness, mentioned in the Bible, is how we see a likeness of Jekyll and Hyde in the life of a believer.

Double-mindedness is a real problem in our society from which Jesus can heal and deliver. Double-mindedness is connected to the psychotic disorder called schizophrenia, where a person's mind and personality become so fragmented and tormented with delusions and instability that eventually he or she becomes unable to function in society.

Schizophrenia sometimes means split personality or split mind. *Schizo* is a Greek word that means "to rend, tear violently, open or unfold."[2] Severe schizophrenia is treated by psychiatry with drugs; as history shows, even shock treatment has been used to treat hallucinations and delusion (mental illness and insanity). There are different degrees of schizophrenia, and most degrees do not require hospitalization.

Although there are many psychiatric and medical definitions of schizophrenia, I am giving the biblical definition based on James 1:8. I use the term double-mindedness because schizophrenia is interpreted by many to be a severe mental illness, and most would not even entertain the idea that they may be schizophrenic.

Psychiatry uses the phrase "an alter ego" (which in Latin means "the other I"), defined as a second self, a second personality or persona within a person who is often oblivious to the persona's actions. This phrase was coined in the early nineteenth century when dissociative identity disorder was first described by psychologists. A person with an alter ego is said to lead a double life. Multiple distinct personalities are called "alters." I believe what psychiatry calls alters are nothing more than demons. Remember, demons have personalities.

Dr. Pat Holliday says, "Double-minded has a psychological, spiritual, emotional and cognitive impact upon the mind. Psychiatrists and Psychologists see it as a mental disorder. Deliverance ministers see it as a spiritual disorder to be resolved through deliverance. The Bible agrees that a person that has a split mind is mentally ill (James 1:8), 'A double-minded man is unstable in all his ways.'"[3]

The majority of double-minded people manage to function in life and have some successes, yet they still have the characteristics of a spirit of schizophrenia. This causes them to be constantly unstable in every area, never having any peace about who they are or what they can or have to accomplish.

They may not always go to a place of insanity that the world describes as schizophrenia.

This revelation of double-mindedness and schizophrenia came to the forefront through the ministry of Frank and Ida Mae Hammond, pioneers in the area of deliverance and authors of the classic book on deliverance *Pigs in the Parlor*. I had the honor of ministering with Frank Hammond and found him to be a humble and gracious servant of the Lord. Before Frank passed away, I asked him to lay hands on me and impart. I believe I received an impartation, and a passion to teach on this subject and see people set free.

THE DIABOLICAL NATURE OF DOUBLE-MINDEDNESS

So who has a problem with double-mindedness? How many people are affected? Frank and Ida Mae Hammond saw double-mindedness as Satan's master plan to destroy the human race. They experienced that "almost every person who comes to us for deliverance is found to have varying degrees of the network of demon spirits which cause schizophrenia."[4] Ida Mae says that "schizophrenia [or double-mindedness] is a disturbance, distortion or disintegration of the development of the personality."[5]

Some will teach that Christians cannot have a spirit of schizophrenia, but please know that when James said that "a double-minded man is unstable in all his ways," he was speaking to the saints (James 1:8).

From *Barnes' Notes on the Bible*:

A double minded man—The word here used is the Greek word dipsuchos, and occurs only here [James 1:8] and in James 4:8. It means, properly, one who has two souls; then one who is wavering or inconstant. It is applicable to a man who has no settled principles; who is controlled by passion; who is influenced by popular feeling; who is now inclined to one opinion or course of conduct, and now to another.[6]

A person in this condition is always wavering, irresolute, doubting, changing, and inconsistent. Synonyms for double-minded include indecisive, inconsistent, unpredictable, erratic, hesitating, vacillating, wavering, procrastinating, questioning, doubting, lingering, delaying, not firmly placed, unsteady, lacking emotional control, and the like. The double-minded man has problems making decisions and sticking with them. Due to his instability, he is always changing his mind concerning relationships, careers, ministries, and churches.

Gill's Exposition of the Entire Bible says it like this:

A double minded man...a man of two souls, or of a double heart, that speaks and asks with an heart, and an heart, as in Psalm 12:2 who halts between two opinions, and is at an uncertainty what to do or say, and is undetermined what to ask for; or who is not sincere and upright in his requests, who asks for one thing, and means another, and asks amiss, and with an ill design; does not call upon God in truth, and in the sincerity of his soul; draws nigh to him with his mouth, and honors him with his lips, but his heart is far from him. Such an one is unstable in all his ways; he is confused in his mind; restless in his thoughts, unsettled in his designs and intentions; inconstant in his petitions; uncertain in his notions and opinion of things; and very variable in his actions, and especially in matters of religion; he is always changing, and never at a point, but at a continual uncertainty, both in a way of thinking and doing: he never continues long either in an opinion, or in a practice, but is ever shifting and moving.[7]

Double-mindedness is the polar opposite of stability, which means not likely to change or fail; firmly established; not easily moved, disturbed, or thrown off balance; firm; steady; not likely to break down, fall apart, or give way; not volatile, or varying infrequently within a narrow range; not subject to mental illness or irrationality; fixed; and firmly established. How many can say that they fit this description in their personality and makeup?

God did not create us to be unstable people. He created us in His image. God is not unstable. He is the same yesterday, today, and forever. God is dependable and consistent. He wants us to be the same. God's purpose is that we have one stable personality and not be torn with multiple personalities. We should not be back and forth like a Ping-Pong ball. We should not be up and down like a yo-yo.

God desires for us to be steadfast and immovable (1 Cor. 15:58). He knows that instability can keep us from excelling.

> Unstable as water, you shall not excel, because you went up to your father's bed; then you defiled it—he went up to my couch.
> —GENESIS 49:4

To excel means to surpass others or be superior in some respect or area; do extremely well.[8] God created us to excel in life. He wants us to excel. We need stability in order to excel.

The desire and plan of the enemy is to cause unbelief, doubt, questioning, reasoning, wavering, and confusion to rule your life. Demons will come to attack you, because the devil knows that without faith it is impossible to please God. Without faith you are unable to receive from God and others, and you will constantly strive to fulfill these voids selfishly and through immediate gratification.

If you lack stable faith, you become double-minded—two opinions, two wars working inside you. These opinions can become two distinct personalities, and though you (your real personality) know you should have faith, faith will not be working fruit in your life as the unstableness of wavering will cause you to be tossed to and fro.

This is why in James 4:8 we learn that those who are double-minded need their hearts purified: "Draw near to God, and He will draw near to you. Cleanse your hands, you sinners, and purify your hearts, you double-minded." As our hearts are purified through deliverance, we grow to love God's Word and hate double-mindedness.

Psalm 119:113 says, "I hate double-minded people, but I love your law" (NIV). According to *Jamieson-Fausset-Brown Bible Commentary*, this verse is literally speaking of "vain thoughts-better, 'unstable persons,' literally, 'divided men,' those of a divided, doubting mind (James 1:8); 'a double-minded man,' skeptics, or, skeptical notions as opposed to the certainty of God's word."[9] As you can see, being double-minded is not a good thing.

These translations of Psalm 119:113 emphasize a hatred for double-mindedness and other ways this spiritual disorder can be described:

> I hate those with *divided loyalties*, but I love your instructions.
>
> —NLT, EMPHASIS ADDED

> I hate *two-faced people*, but I love your teachings.
>
> —GW, EMPHASIS ADDED

You cannot be double-minded and love the Word at the same time. Double-mindedness will draw you away from the Word. There are many with divided loyalties. We must hate double-mindedness and fall out of agreement with it. We must submit to deliverance, and this will happen if we hate double-mindedness and desire to be free.

How Double-Mindedness Gets In

Two main strongholds make up the double-minded personality—rejection and rebellion—with the root of bitterness coming in secondarily. They interact like a threefold cord and are not easily broken.

Rejection is the doorway to double-mindedness. Demons associated with rejection make it almost impossible for a person to develop into the true person God created them to be. They become ruled by these spirits and find themselves always trying to compensate for their lack of development and lack of confidence. Next they become rebellious to protect themselves from hurt and being taken advantage of. With rebellion comes bitterness—bitterness held against people and life circumstances that have caused all kinds of hurt and trauma.

Double-mindedness is a dangerous, demonic spirit that causes people to be tossed around like Ping-Pong balls, going between the two false (demonic) personalities (inward then outward). Double-minded people are always in a state of instability. They go back and forth between the rejection personality and the rebellion personality.

As we have already begun to discuss, double-mindedness is common to us all. Without deliverance from God, we all will deal with recurring double-mindedness.

We live in a world of instability. There are unstable people, mothers, fathers, families, leaders, churches, nations, governments, and economies. If you are unstable, and live with unstable people, you will be a storm within a storm. You must have a stable personality and an unshakeable foundation in God in order to live in an unstable world. Deliverance and developing a godly identity are the solutions to this growing problem.

Over the next several chapters, I will break down how double-mindedness takes root in a believer's life, give examples of how it shows up throughout the Bible, uncover the clusters of demons associated with this personality, and explain how to get delivered and become a stable, unshakeable believer.

My prayer is that this book will open your understanding to the subject of double-mindedness and provide keys for lasting deliverance, healing, restoration, and victory. No believer should remain in a place where he or she can't receive from the Lord.

> Therefore, my beloved brothers, be steadfast, unmovable, always abounding in the work of the Lord, knowing that your labor in the Lord is not in vain.
> —1 CORINTHIANS 15:58

CHAPTER 2

UNSTABLE IN ALL THEIR WAYS

Double-Mindedness in Everyday Life

He who wavers is like a wave of the sea, driven and tossed with the wind. Let not that man think that he will receive anything from the Lord. A double-minded man is unstable in all his ways.

—JAMES 1:6–8

W E ALL KNOW people, including ourselves, who act at times in polar opposites. The minister who is godly, prayerful, and holy at times yet has periods of sin and perversion. The believer who lives a strong Christian life but has seasons of backsliding. The person who is outgoing and cheerful yet falls into bouts of withdrawal and depression. The person who is hard working and a perfectionist yet has periods of lethargy and sloppiness. The person who is gentle and kind but has periods of outburst and rage. It is almost as if you are dealing with two people. This is double-mindedness.

The Greek phrase for "double-minded" (*dipsuchos*) literally means "double souled," from *dis*, meaning "twice," and *psuche*, meaning "mind."[1] Having two minds is the description of confusion. Confusion is a lack of understanding; uncertainty, a situation of panic; a breakdown of order.

Double-mindedness can result in a lifetime of bad relationships. Relationships and covenants require stability. Unstable people will have a difficult time with long-lasting, stable relationships. This affects marriages as well and is the real cause of many divorces. This instability affects families and children, who need stable parents and a stable home environment in which to grow. It affects churches, because churches are fellowships that require strong and loving relationships. What is even more tragic is that double-mindedness can affect a person's relationship with God.

Let's take a closer look now into how double-mindedness and instability affect every area of our lives. Knowing is half the battle in spiritual warfare and deliverance.

How Double-Mindedness
Affects Our Daily Lives

Where do wars and fights among you come from? Do they not come from your lusts that war in your body? You lust and do not have, so you kill. You desire to have and cannot obtain. You fight and war. Yet you do not have, because you do not ask. You ask, and do not receive, because you ask amiss, that you may spend it on your passions.

You adulterers and adulteresses, do you not know that the friendship with the world is enmity with God? Whoever therefore will be a friend of the world is the enemy of God. Do you think that the Scripture says in vain, "He yearns jealously for the spirit that lives in us"? But He gives more grace. For this reason it says: "God resists the proud, but gives grace to the humble."

Therefore submit yourselves to God. Resist the devil, and he will flee from you. Draw near to God, and He will draw near to you. Cleanse your hands, you sinners, and purify your hearts, you double-minded. Grieve and mourn and weep. Let your laughter be turned to mourning, and your joy to dejection. Humble yourselves in the sight of the Lord, and He will lift you up.

—James 4:1–10

Reading the full context of how James 4:8 fits into the complete message the apostle James is trying to convey gives us a better idea of how double-mindedness shows up in our lives. Even when we look like lovers of God on the outside, our passions can be at war within us. James goes on to say that friendship with the world makes a person an enemy of God. That sounds like the last thing anyone would want to be. To be double-minded is to try to be religious and love God, and simultaneously chase after passions in the world. Out of this dichotomy comes things we see in our lives and relationships from our home lives to public interactions, both small scale to large scale and everything in between.

War and fighting

> Where do wars and fights among you come from? Do
> they not come from your lusts that war in your body?
> —JAMES 4:1

Wars and fighting come from lust. Lust is a part of the rejection personality. Lust causes confusion. This is the hurricane of double-mindedness.

Worldliness and carnality

> You adulterers and adulteresses, do you not know that the
> friendship with the world is enmity with God? Whoever
> therefore will be a friend of the world is the enemy of God.
> —JAMES 4:4

The rejection side of the double-minded personality weds a person to the world for love. It is simply Satan's substitute for true love. Double-mindedness breeds worldliness and carnality.

Worldliness can be seen in teenage rebellion. Teenagers will often get involved in a lifestyle of lust, perversion, drugs, etc. Parents are often at their wits' end. Signs of double-mindedness can be seen in piercings, tattoos, punk dressing, Goth dressing, provocative clothing, drug addiction, smoking, running away, fighting, gang activity, profanity, disrespect to authority, alternative lifestyles, depression, suicidal tendencies, and withdrawal.

> For a generation now, disruptive young Americans who rebel against authority figures have been increasingly diagnosed with mental illnesses and medicated with psychiatric (psychotropic) drugs. Disruptive young people who are medicated with Ritalin, Adderall, and other amphetamines routinely report that these drugs make them "care less" about their boredom, resentments, and other negative emotions, thus making them more compliant and manageable. And so-called atypical antipsychotics such as Risperdal and Zyprexa—powerful tranquilizing drugs—are increasingly prescribed to disruptive young Americans, even though in most cases they are not displaying any psychotic symptoms.[2]

Teenage double-mindedness has become an epidemic. Most don't know what they are dealing with. God's solution is deliverance and healing. Double-mindedness has also been called passive-aggression, but it is simply rejection/rebellion.

Indecision

> If it is displeasing to you to serve the Lord, then *choose* today whom you will serve, if it should be the gods your fathers served beyond the River or the gods of the Amorites' land where you are now living. Yet as for me and my house, we will serve the LORD.
> —JOSHUA 24:15, EMPHASIS ADDED

Double-mindedness causes indecision, which results in procrastination, compromise, confusion, forgetfulness, and indifference. Indecision is one of the most debilitating problems in life because life is based on decisions. Indifference is an attitude that causes a person to avoid making decisions. Procrastination is another way of avoiding decisions by just putting them off for a future time. It can also be rooted in the fear of making a decision. In addition to this is the fear of making the *wrong* choice.

Our choices pave the way for success or failure. A double-minded person has a difficult time making decisions and often changes his or her mind after making a decision. This results in wavering and always questioning one's own decisions.

> I call heaven and earth to witnesses against you this day, that I have set before you life and death, blessing and curse. Therefore choose life, that both you and your descendants may live.
> —Deuteronomy 30:19

The Word of God challenges us to make wise decisions. We are commanded to choose life. We can choose blessing or cursing. We can choose the fear of the Lord. We can choose to serve the Lord.

Our life is the result of our choices. We choose our paths in life. We choose whom we marry. When we have children, we influence what they will choose as they get older. We choose the jobs we will work, the friends we will have, and the places we will live. The Bible is filled with examples of men and women who made bad choices and suffered the consequences. It also shows us the blessing of wise choices.

The double-minded person is often paralyzed when it comes to making choices. Have you ever been around those who can't decide what they want to do in life? It is frustrating to say the least. This can be a sign of double-mindedness and the need for deliverance. Proper decision making is the result of wisdom and a stable personality.

DOUBLE-MINDEDNESS IN OUR FAMILIES

Double-mindedness affects our ability to honor and stay true to covenant. Covenant requires stability, loyalty, and faithfulness. How can we walk in covenant if we are double-minded? How can we have strong covenant relationships if we are double-minded? God is a covenant-keeping God, and our relationship with Him is based on covenant.

Marriage is a covenant between a husband and a wife. Is it any wonder that we have so many divorces in and out of the church? There are too many unstable people entering into marriages. Double-minded people will have instability in their marriages. We will continue to see troubled marriages unless double-mindedness is dealt with. With such a large number of marriages ending in divorce, it is no surprise that double-mindedness is a major problem.

A word to husbands and fathers

There are a lot of double-minded men who are married and have children. Families need strong, steadfast men. Men are called to be the providers and protectors of the family. When trouble comes, the husband and father should be able to stand up and say, "Honey, I got this. Don't worry, baby. Children, don't worry. It's all right. I believe God. I pray. I bind. I loose. I take authority over the devil. I'm the head of my house. Devil, you cannot have my wife, my kids, or my family. You will not destroy us, because I trust in God. I am the covering. I am the head of this house."

Yet too frequently we find weak, double-minded men who let their wives go to church and do all the praying and believing, while they stay home watching football. Then when spiritual trouble comes they don't know how to pray, bind the devil, loose, stand up for anything, or recite a scripture. They leave their families vulnerable to attack.

Kingdom families need godly men who will stand up and say, "I fear the Lord. My heart is fixed. I will not be moved. I'm a godly man. I'm not double-minded. I am single-minded. I've already made the decision. I am established in God. I am not wavering. I am not doubting. I believe God. I take the shield of faith, and I quench every fiery dart of the wicked one. I am not an Ahab, double-minded man."

I especially challenge men to take hold of the message in this book. I challenge men to stand up and be single-minded. Get healed and delivered from double-mindedness and allow God to stabilize you so that your personality will become mature in Christ. As I will discuss in the last chapter on the Psalm 112 believer, you can be the man who does not fear evil tidings because your heart is fixed, trusting in the Lord. Set your heart upon God. Make the clear decision to serve God and love Him with all your heart. Be a man of God. Love His Word. Love His Spirit. Love what is right and holy. Love the things of God. Declare that you will not be ashamed to be a man of God in all your ways, never compromising.

Other men may waver and be drunkards, whoremongers, liars, and cheaters. Other men may not want to get married, raise their children, or keep covenant. But that is not who you have to be, man of God. That is not what you should want to do. You can be a man of God who loves his wife, loves his children, loves people, is holy and clean, loves to pray, loves to worship, loves to sing, and loves to talk about the things of God. Yes, you can be a man of God whose heart is fixed. You can know who you are. You can be sure of what you believe and in whom you have believed. You can be stable.

DOUBLE-MINDEDNESS AND YOUR PHYSICAL HEALTH

> A merry heart does good like a medicine, but a broken spirit dries the bones.
>
> —PROVERBS 17:22

Chris Simpson of New Wine Media teaches on the effects that the double-minded stronghold of rejection can have on a person's physical health. He says:

> Did you know that rejection can affect you physically? It can dry up your bones. Generally, it's the "internalizers" that tend to get sick from their rejection. Why is that? It's because rejection often produces anger. And you have to do something with your anger. If you bury it inside, it'll find a way to the surface. If you live in denial concerning your anger, then you'll be resentful and bitter. These attitudes can bring physical problems.
>
> I've often seen people healed on the spot when they forgave those that had hurt them, and when they renounced the bitterness and resentment in their heart. It's amazing how quickly the Holy Spirit will heal and bring life to the dried bones. Many sicknesses and physical maladies tend to be rooted in rejection and bitterness: skin problems, headaches, allergies, neck or back aches, stiffness of joints, arthritis, pains, stress, nervousness, and various diseases.[3]

What he shares here I have seen as well in my almost forty years of deliverance ministry. When I have laid hands on an individual to bring deliverance from bitterness, anger, and unforgiveness, I have found that rejection and rebellion are at the root of their issues. They often get healed from various physical ailments such as heart disease, some cancers, arthritis, and more when they forgive and release bitterness.

I will go in depth about the correlation between double-mindedness and the spirit of infirmity in a later chapter. But know that rejection can lead to self-rejection, which will manifest as illness in the body. We are seeing a rise of autoimmune disease diagnosis, and the cause for much of it is unknown. Autoimmune diseases occur when the immune system begins to attack the body. Thyroiditis, arthritis, type 1 diabetes, certain cancers and heart diseases, lupus, various allergies, and asthma are kinds of autoimmune diseases. Autoimmune symptoms often manifest after a person experiences a devastating loss, endures trauma, or is excessively stressed over a period of time.

Double-Mindedness in the Church

The stronghold of double-mindedness runs rampant in our churches. The cycle of rejection and rebellion and then bitterness destroys churches. People fall away from churches because of rejection from leadership. Leaders fall out of agreement because of rejection and rebellion, which leads to church splits. We have all witnessed or experienced the effects of double-mindedness in church.

There is too much hurt and bitterness in the church. There are too many offended leaders and believers. This is why so many believers feel that their church doesn't operate in the supernatural with signs and wonders and healings and deliverance. The power of God cannot be sustained in any church that is filled with so much bitterness. Unforgiveness and bitterness will stop a move of God. These things harden people's hearts and make it impossible for the Spirit of God to have free course. The Bible says that God is nigh unto them with a contrite spirit. (See Psalm 34:18.) Brokenness and repentance are necessary. You cannot have revival when bitterness is in the hearts of believers. Bitterness is a poison that will contaminate a church.

This is why the deliverance ministry is so needed today. Hebrews 12:15 says, "watching diligently so that no one falls short of the grace of God, lest any root of bitterness spring up to cause trouble, and many become defiled by it."

Let's look at other ways double-mindedness affects our church lives.

Spirit of rebellion and church splits

Absalom is the biblical picture of the spirit of rebellion. He was a son of King David. The major parts of his story are told in 2 Samuel 13–19. Absalom was full of hate, revenge, and murder after his brother Amnon raped their half sister, Tamar. He must have felt that justice would not have been sought on behalf of his sister, and he was probably right. Things were different for women then. Absalom shared his sister's shame, guilt, rejection, hurt, and bitterness. The Bible says that he waited two years to get revenge on his brother (2 Sam. 13:23–29). This means that for two years he seethed with hate and bitterness against his brother. Finally he had his men do his dirty work, and they killed Amnon. Then Absalom went into hiding for fear of his father.

During Absalom's exile, David did not go see him. Yet the king's general, Joab, advocated for Absalom before the king and asked if Absalom could be allowed to live in his own home in Jerusalem again. The king granted this request but still did not go to visit his son or summon him into his presence.

Absalom once again leaned on Joab to advocate for him, and finally David granted his request. But by this time a spirit of rejection had already set into Absalom's heart. He came into Jerusalem and began to stir seeds of distrust and discord among the people in the kingdom. In 2 Samuel 15:2–6, it says:

> Absalom would go early and stand beside the way into the gate. When any man who had a dispute concerning which he had come to the king for a judgment approached, Absalom would call to him and say, "Which city are you from?" And he would say, "Your servant is from one of the tribes of Israel." Then Absalom would say to him, "Look, your claim is good and right, but there is no one to hear you on behalf of the king." Absalom would continue, "If I were appointed a judge in the land, then every man who had a claim could come and I would give him justice."...Absalom acted this way toward every Israelite who came to the king for a judgment. So Absalom stole the hearts of the men of Israel.

After repeated actions like this, Absalom won the hearts of the people. He established himself as a leader in their eyes behind David's back. After four years Absalom determined to take the people who had pledged their loyalty to him to another city, Hebron, and have himself declared king over them. His numbers grew so much that David feared for his own life and fled Jerusalem. When David left Jerusalem, the coast was clear for Absalom to return from Hebron as king. He attempted to usurp David's anointed position as king over Israel, but he did not succeed.

David was able to gather his own troops who remained loyal and was forced to launch a counterattack against his own son. In the end Absalom was hung in a tree by his hair. David's general, Joab, found him there and killed him. Absalom's rebellion wreaked a lot havoc and caused a huge split in the nation of Israel.

This is what double-mindedness can do in a church. Leaders or members in a church can be hurt or offended by other leaders or members. It starts with rejection, then moves to rebellion, and finally bitterness drives them to seek to destroy the whole church, like Absalom tried to destroy the kingdom.

Based on what we've just seen from Absalom's life, there are twelve stages individuals go through when they become influenced by the spirit of rebellion. The following traits are seen in many churches and organizations when this spirit is not dealt with:[4]

1. Independent spirit—An attitude of independence emerges when the person no longer wants to serve the leadership but seeks recognition and a reputation.

2. Self-promotion—The person will maneuver for the praise of men. In 2 Samuel 15 Absalom stole the hearts of the people.

3. Spiritual pride—As people recognize and praise the deceived individual, he begins to believe that he is more spiritual than the leaders.

4. Offended spirit—When the leadership does not promote the rebellious person's ideas and gifts as he believes they should, he becomes highly offended. He is full of pride and often will seek others who will agree with him and his offense.

5. Critical spirit—Like Absalom with his father, David, the rebellious person questions and undermines almost all the leaders' decisions in front of the people. Because of this critical spirit, the rebellious person no longer receives any spiritual feeding or direction from the leadership.

6. Competitive spirit—The rebellious person sets himself in competition with leadership and begins to distort and misrepresent the decisions and directives the leaders are giving.

7. Strife and division—The rebellious person will take his offenses to many individuals in the church or organization and spread his discontent through various means.

8. Accusing the leadership—The critical and fault-finding spirit manifests again at this stage by the rebellious person harping on the minor things he finds wrong with the leadership. These things are not usually related to God's spiritual qualifications—he criticizes what kind of car the

pastor drives, how long he takes to receive the offerings, etc. He feeds these things to those who have joined his bandwagon to gain more loyalty.

9. Open disloyalty and division—At this stage the rebellious person feels that he has enough support to bring his disloyalty and rebellion out in the open. The leaders become aware of the division, and now those who have bought in to the rebellion are forced to make a choice between the leaders and the Absalom who deceived them.

10. Bold conspiracy—The rebellious person justifies his conspiracy to everyone by focusing his attention on all the minor faults within the leadership. Usually these issues are not legitimate. They are not on the level of things such as the leaders preaching false doctrines or their being involved in blatant sin.

11. Church split—This is where the leader of the rebellion leads a naive splinter group out to birth a new church, ministry, or organization. They launch out to declare a new vision.

12. God's judgment on the rebellious church—The Bible says, "If the root be evil, the whole tree will be evil." (See Matthew 12:33.) Every organization that is started by a person with an Absalom spirit will be full of rebellion, disloyalty, and continual splits.

Ruled by bitterness and pride, the Absalom spirit of rebellion will try to gain influence through deception, flattery, and treachery. Pastor Chew Weng Chee further outlines the six-step progression this spirit takes in spreading throughout a church or organization. We must be aware when we see these steps begin to take place:[5]

1. The Absalom spirit plants doubts and casts slurs on God's ordained leadership. They criticize the pastors or leaders, saying that they don't care, that they don't develop you.

2. The Absalom spirit uses kindness, handouts and favors as their means to gain the hearts of the people. They take effort to carefully construct an image to impress.

3. The Absalom spirit needs an audience to thrive. It will speak to 2,000 people but not two. If there is no audience, it goes somewhere else. They look for people in want, discontented people, and those who are anti-establishment. They are very dangerous.

4. The Absalom makes promises he does not intend to keep.

5. Unforgiveness and bitterness are the underlying causes for this type of spirit to germinate. Some people are hurt and offended that the pastor hurt them, that the [small group leader] hurt them. We are called to forgive, and not give room for the Absalom spirit to work. It thrives on offenses. We need to forgive and move on with our focus to build God's kingdom. [Unfortunately this is not what many believers do.]

6. The Absalom spirit is able to deceive even the elect and bring them over to his side. Ahithophel was David's wisest counselor. Even he was deceived. His betrayal affected David most significantly. [See 2 Samuel 15:31–35.]

Unbelief and backsliding

Now the just shall live by faith; but if anyone draws back, My soul shall have no pleasure in him.

—HEBREWS 10:38

Unbelief and backsliding are other things I have seen as a pattern in many believers. I have seen believers commit to Christ and then turn away and return to the world. They then return and repeat the process over again. This is heartbreaking. Unbelief and backsliding are signs of double-mindedness, wavering between two lifestyles. They were also the issues of those in the early church who were departing from the faith. Many of the Hebrews were returning to the old covenant system. They were wavering in their faith. Wavering is a sign of double-mindedness.

These Christians were also fighting and warring with one another, and James commanded them to humble themselves and cleanse their hands (James 4). Notice in this same passage that the spirits of lust and pride are prevalent in the double-minded, and there is contention, strife, and adultery. Adultery is unfaithfulness to covenant and can refer to backsliding and apostasy. Some of these believers were leaving Christ and returning to the world; James referred to them as sinners (v. 8).

Double-mindedness breeds unbelief and doubt. Backsliding and apostasy can be signs of double-mindedness. The prophet

Jeremiah revealed that the remedy to backsliding is healing—
or, in other words, deliverance (Jer. 3:22).

Are you double-minded in your walk with Christ? Do you
have a history of backsliding and departing from the faith? Are
you guilty of worldliness and carnality? Do you crack under
pressure or persecution and return to the things of the world?
These are all signs of double-mindedness.

The double-minded are not stable enough to deal with the
challenges that often come with being a believer. They will
often withdraw or rebel. We must become stable if we are to
walk with God consistently. Deliverance is the answer, and I
am committed to seeing this truth taught in the church.

A closer look at backsliding in the Old and New Testaments

The Hebrew words for the term *backsliding* are *mshu-
wbah*, meaning "apostasy: backsliding, turning away,"[6] and
sarar, meaning "to turn away, i.e. (morally) be refractory—X
away, backsliding, rebellious, revolter(-ing), slide back, stubborn, withdrew."[7] Other words from the Hebrew, *shobab* and
shobeb, render the English meanings "apostate, i.e. idolatrous—
backsliding, frowardly, turn away (from margin);" "heathenish
or (actually) heathen—backsliding."[8]

Israel was a double-minded nation, going in and out of covenant with God. They were not consistent in their loyalty to
God. I will talk specifically about what their journey with God
can teach us in another chapter, but I want to highlight some
things here as examples of what their journey shows us about
inconsistent faith and obedience to God in our lives.

Israel was guilty of revolt, rebellion, turning away, stubbornness, idolatry, and acting like the heathen nations that

surrounded it. This leaves me no doubt that chronic back-sliding is a manifestation of double-mindedness.

Stop sliding

Consider these translations of Psalm 26:1:

> Vindicate me, O LORD, for I have walked in my integrity, and I have trusted in the LORD without wavering.
>
> —NAS

> Judge me, O LORD; for I have walked in mine integrity: I have trusted also in the LORD; therefore I shall not slide.
>
> —KJV

> Judge me, O Jehovah, for I have walked in mine integrity: I have trusted also in Jehovah without wavering.
>
> —ASV

> Judge me, O Jehovah, for I have walked in mine integrity, and I have confided in Jehovah: I shall not slip.
>
> —DARBY

> By David. Judge me, O Jehovah, for I in mine integrity have walked, and in Jehovah I have trusted, I slide not.
>
> —YLT

The Hebrew word used in this verse for "slide," "slip," or "waver" is *maad*, also meaning "make to shake."[9]

Shortly after the coming of the Holy Spirit on the Day of Pentecost, many believers were strengthened and held fast to the apostles' doctrine, fellowship, breaking of bread, and prayers. (See Acts 2:42.) This is the opposite of being double-minded.

As the believers grew in number and in faith, persecution grew and caused discouragement. They were warned against falling from steadfastness: "You therefore, beloved, since you know these things beforehand, beware lest you also fall from your own firm footing, being led away by the deception of the wicked" (2 Pet. 3:17).

Strong's defines steadfastness using the Greek words *stereóma* and *stérigmos*, both meaning "something established, i.e. (abstractly) confirmation (stability)—steadfastness;" "stability (figuratively)—steadfastness."[10]

When the letter of James was written, there was great suffering among the early Christians, and there were many whose faithfulness was waning. Many were departing from the faith and being double-minded in their walk with God. Apostasy was a major problem in the early church, and this was the result of double-mindedness. James encouraged them to remain steadfast in the New Covenant and their commitment to Christ.

As an example, the Colossian church was commended for their steadfastness.

> For though I am absent in the flesh, yet I am with you in spirit, rejoicing and seeing your orderliness and the steadfastness of your faith in Christ.
>
> —COLOSSIANS 2:5

In James 1:6 we see a picture of a storm:

> But let him ask in faith, without wavering. For he who wavers is like a wave of the sea, driven and tossed with the wind.

This is what double-mindedness looks like—a storm, a hurricane. When two unstable people collide, it is like a storm within a storm. Do you have a history of stormy relationships?

Is the church filled with stormy marriages? Are there always storms in your church and ministry? If the answer is yes, then the problem is double-mindedness.

False ministers who twist the Scriptures

> As in all his letters, he writes about these things, in which some things are hard to understand, which the unlearned and *unstable* distort, as they also do the other Scriptures, to their own destruction.
>
> —2 PETER 3:16, EMPHASIS ADDED

Unstable, double-minded ministers twist the Scriptures. Unstable people cannot handle the meat of the Word. I am convinced that cults are led by double-minded leaders—unstable leaders followed by unstable people. Unstable leaders are also controlling, which is a part of the rebellion personality.

This is the characteristic of false apostles and ministers in general:

> For such are false apostles and deceitful workers, disguising themselves as apostles of Christ…For you permit it if a man brings you into bondage, if a man devours you, if a man takes from you, if a man exalts himself, or if a man strikes you on the face.
>
> —2 CORINTHIANS 11:13, 20

False ministers exalt themselves and smite you on the face. They are abusive and controlling. These are all signs of the rebellion personality (similar to what has been taught about the Jezebel spirit).

False ministers are also deceived. They operate in false deception and delusion with false revelations. Deception and delusion are parts of rebellion. Witchcraft (control, possessiveness) is also a part of rebellion.

Unstable people are attracted to cults and legalistic, controlling churches because they are looking for identity. When an individual doesn't have an identity, she will find one by getting with what she considers a "special" group. She will find herself under the control of unstable, false leaders who are also double-minded.

Unstable preachers have too many issues. There are too many people whose identities are wrapped up in being apostles, prophets, evangelists, bishops, and so forth. They often twist the Scriptures and come up with all kinds of "revelations." I have consistently seen this problem in ministry. The lack of deliverance in the church is the reason why we see so many unhealed double-minded people, even among leadership. Beware of being in a "Saul" ministry, which I will discuss more in the next chapter.

We must make sure that the leaders in our ministries are stable people. Gifting is not the only requirement. Character is important. The more we know about double-mindedness, the more we can identify it within ourselves and receive deliverance. We cannot allow confusion to run rampant in the church.

As we move into this next chapter, which talks about where double-mindedness shows up in the Bible, perhaps the Holy Spirit is beginning to show you some double-minded tendencies in your life. The Lord may be calling you to have more stability in certain areas. Do not dismiss the conviction of the Lord. He chastens those He loves. It is God's love and grace that calls us to repentance. Through repentance and deliverance we are able to establish our sure footing in Him. We are able to walk upright in Him and receive the full benefits of being His child.

I encourage you to continue through the next parts of this book with prayer and a contrite heart, open to the Spirit of God. He may want to show you things about yourself that, if you receive healing in those areas, could cause you to be catapulted to the next level.

> Create in me a clean heart, O God, and renew a right spirit within me...The sacrifices of God are a broken spirit; a broken and a contrite heart, O God, You will not despise.
> —PSALM 51:10, 17

CHAPTER 3

STUCK BETWEEN TWO OPINIONS

Double-Mindedness in the Bible

Elijah came to all the people and said, "How long will you stay between two opinions? If the LORD is God, follow Him, but if Baal, then follow him." And the people did not say a word.

—1 KINGS 18:21

T HE TERM *DOUBLE-MINDED* only appears twice in the whole New Testament. Once in James 1:8—"A double-minded man is unstable in all his ways"—and another time in

James 4:8: "Draw near to God, and He will draw near to you. Cleanse your hands, you sinners, and purify your hearts, you double-minded."

But there are many more living illustrations of double-mindedness throughout the Bible that give us insight into how this demonic spirit manifests and sabotages our lives. We are going to look at quite a few Old Testament examples. Much of what we will uncover in this chapter may not be new to you—Israel's rebellion and idolatry, Saul's fall from grace, and Jezebel and Ahab—but you may not have studied these stories in connection with double-mindedness.

The revelation these examples bring to understanding double-mindedness is the key to seeing how deep the root of this stronghold goes into the sin nature of man. To see how insidious the enemy is in contriving traps and bondages for God's people will build in you a strong desire to see you and all those you know set free from his grip. Let's start off this study with looking at the nation of Israel.

ISRAEL: A DOUBLE-MINDED NATION

Israel was guilty of double-mindedness. Elijah confronted the Israelites on Mount Carmel and demanded they make a choice. Israel was guilty of rebellion throughout their history. They had gone back and forth between worshipping God and worshipping idols. Their loyalties were divided. They were not consistent in keeping their covenant with God. The prophets confronted this rebellion, and in 1 Kings 18:21 Elijah pointed out their inconsistency. The New International Version of this verse says, "How long will you waver between two opinions?" Israel was wavering. And it was at this juncture, this showdown at Mount Carmel between the prophet of God and the 450 prophets of Baal, that God demanded through His prophet that they make a decision and stick with it.

Referring back to the King James Version of 1 Kings 18:21, we find a literal picture of what Elijah was communicating to the people of Israel:

> The term "halt you" in the King James Version ("falter," NKJV)...suggests a person staggering, unable to catch his balance, and failing to accomplish anything of any consequence because his mind is divided. The person in such a circumstance cannot get a grip on life. These people were wavering back and forth, which was typical of the Israelites. The Bible shows in many places that the people continued to worship God, yet also served their idols. In Exodus 32, the incident of the Golden Calf, the people had Aaron mold a calf of gold and proclaim a feast to the Lord!
>
> Essentially, they tried to syncretize the true God and pagan idols, which suggests a divided mind. "No man can serve two masters; for...he will hate the one and love the other" (Matthew 6:24). But the one that he hates is still a part of his mind, and it will cause problems.
>
> In Elijah's word-picture, he is indicating that though nothing is wrong with the rest of the body, because the mind has no focus, the body's efforts have no direction. This sets up a situation where, at best, there will be little movement—that is, little accomplished—and at worst, there will be no forward movement at all, but just staggering, first this way then that. That sort of situation produces nothing.[1]

In Matthew 22:37–38 the Israelites were commanded to love the Lord with all their heart, soul, and mind. This is the opposite of double-mindedness. This was the first and great commandment Israel never kept.

The Bible says in Joshua 24:15, "If it is displeasing to you to serve the LORD, then choose today whom you will serve, if it should be the gods your fathers served beyond the River or the gods of the Amorites' land where you are now living. Yet as for me and my house, we will serve the LORD." Here we can see that God wanted Israel to make a choice. Joshua is a picture of single-mindedness, and he made the choice for himself and his house to serve the Lord. There was no wavering on his part. He was resolute and firm in his decision.

Israel as a whole did not make this choice. They wavered. They were inconsistent. Israel showed all the classic signs of double-mindedness. Their example shows that even a group of people can be double-minded.

Israel's beginning was one of rejection. Notice these words:

> Thus says the Lord GOD to Jerusalem: Your birth and your nativity are from the land of Canaan. Your father was an Amorite, and your mother a Hittite. As for your birth, on the day you were born your navel cord was not cut, nor were you washed in water to cleanse you. You were not rubbed with salt, nor wrapped in swaddling cloths. No eye pitied you to do any of these to you, to have compassion on you. But you were cast out in the open field, to the loathing of your person, in the day that you were born.
>
> When I passed by you and saw you polluted in your own blood, I said to you when you were in your blood, "Live!" Indeed, I said to you when you were in your blood, "Live!"
>
> —EZEKIEL 16:3–6

The prophet Ezekiel describes Israel as a child rejected from birth. God pitied her, had compassion on her, and caused her to live. Israel survived as a nation because of God's love and care. Yet when Israel grew, she played the harlot.

> You trusted in your own beauty, and played the harlot because of your renown, and poured out your fornications on every willing passerby.
>
> —Ezekiel 16:15

This is the classic behavior of a person who was rejected at a young age by his or her parents. This person does not have any sure footing on how to deal with the feeling of being unwanted and cast aside. Rejection can lead to self-rejection, which is demonstrated in the verse above. It is not uncommon to find that a person who is promiscuous, careless with himself or herself, or uses his or her body or physical features to gain some kind of affection or approval has experienced some form of parental rejection, usually rejection from the father. Even when you try to help a person with these issues, it seems that there is nothing you can do to heal the invisible wounds of the heart. This is where deliverance comes in.

God shows that Israel had been rejected from the womb. This rejection was acted out as rebellion, even against a God who loved them. Israel's rebellion brought God's judgement. Israel was guilty of covenant violations and continually broke the covenant. Israel's relationship with God was severed by rebellion.

In Isaiah 1:2 God voices His testimony against Israel: "Hear, O heavens, and give ear, O earth. For the LORD has spoken: I have nourished and brought up children, and they have rebelled against Me." The Israelites rebelled against the One who nourished and brought them up. They were inconsistent and never fully lived up to their covenant responsibilities. They were unfaithful. They were covenant breakers.

The Book of Judges details Israel's double-mindedness. Israel would sin, go into captivity, call upon the Lord, be delivered, walk with God for a season, and then repeat the cycle over again.

There were also reformations and revivals throughout Israel's history. These were only temporary until finally God allowed them to go into Babylon. The relationship between God and Israel was up and down. The difference between God and Israel was that God was the faithful partner. God's mercy upon His covenant people was steadfast. God is not double-minded.

Israel was not steadfast (devoted, committed):

> And they might not be as their fathers, a stubborn and rebellious generation, a generation that did not set their heart steadfast, and whose spirit was not faithful to God.
> —PSALM 78:8

> For their heart was not devoted to Him, neither were they committed to His covenant.
> —PSALM 78:37

But God was steadfast (enduring):

> I make a decree that in every dominion of my kingdom men are to fear and tremble before the God of Daniel. "For He is the living God, enduring forever; His kingdom shall never be destroyed, and His dominion shall be forever."
> —DANIEL 6:26

God was single-minded in His devotion and loyalty to Israel, but Israel was double-minded in her devotion and loyalty toward God. *Steadfast* is defined as resolutely or dutifully firm and unwavering: "steadfast loyalty," steady, unwavering or determined in purpose, loyalty, etc.[2] To be steadfast means to be firm, steady, stiff, unbendable, unfaltering, unshakeable, unwavering, committed, devoted, enduring, and faithful. This is the opposite of double-mindedness. God's covenant love and loyalty to Israel was unwavering. Israel's covenant love and loyalty to God was always inconsistent and wavering. This is double-mindedness, always wavering, inconsistent, and unfaithful. Israel was the opposite of God's character of faithfulness—disloyal, unreliable, and untrustworthy.

In Deuteronomy 30:19 God called Israel out again, demanding that the people make a choice: "I call heaven and earth to witnesses against you this day, that I have set before you life and death, blessing and curse. Therefore choose life, that both you and your descendants may live." Their ability to make a decision and stick with it was a matter of life and death.

Life and death are choices. God commanded Israel to choose life. There was no room for double-mindedness. The double-minded person is always wavering between the two.

Let's take a look now at Saul, one of Israel's kings.

SAUL—HOW DOUBLE-MINDEDNESS MANIFESTS AS FEAR

King Saul is a biblical example of paranoia. He became paranoid of those around him, especially David, and accused them of conspiring to take his kingdom.

> You have all conspired against me, and no one revealed
> to me that my son made a covenant with the son of Jesse.
> And not one of you is grieved for me and revealed it to me
> that my son raised up my servant against me to ambush
> me as at this day.
>
> —1 SAMUEL 22:8

Notice Saul also manifested self-pity in saying that no one was sorry for him. The person that is the target of this manifestation of double-mindedness is often perplexed when his motives are judged for no reason.

Because of paranoia and fear, Saul also became suspicious. Read here in 1 Samuel 18:6–9:

> When they came home, as David was returning from
> slaying the Philistine, the women came out from all cities
> of Israel to meet King Saul, singing and dancing, with
> tambourines, with joy, and with musical instruments.
> The dancing women sang and said, "Saul has slain his
> thousands, and David his ten thousands."
>
> Saul became very angry, and this saying was displeasing to him. Therefore he said, "They have ascribed
> to David ten thousands, but to me they have ascribed
> thousands. Now what remains for him to have but the
> kingdom?"
>
> So Saul was suspicious of David from that day and
> forward.

David had done nothing to deserve this. He was faithful to Saul, and now Saul was suspicious of his motives. David became the target of Saul's paranoia.

Double-minded leaders need deliverance. Leaders who are suspicious of everyone around them will use their power and authority to destroy the targets of their suspicion. Saul eventually tried to murder David.

Have you ever been around someone who was suspicious of everyone? They think everyone is out to get them. They don't trust anyone. This can be a sign of instability and double-mindedness.

Saul's fear ultimately led him to disobedience and even caused him to his lose his kingdom:

> Samuel said, "Does the LORD delight in burnt offerings and sacrifices as much as in obeying the voice of the LORD? Obedience is better than sacrifice, a listening ear than the fat of rams. For rebellion is as the sin of witchcraft, and stubbornness is as iniquity and idolatry. Because you have rejected the word of the LORD, He has also rejected you from being king."
>
> Saul said to Samuel, "I have sinned. For I have transgressed the commandment of the LORD, and your words, because I feared the people, and obeyed their voice. Now therefore, please pardon my sin and return with me, that I may worship the LORD."
>
> Samuel said to Saul, "I will not return with you. For you have rejected the word of the LORD, and the LORD has rejected you from being king over Israel."
> —1 SAMUEL 15:22–26

In this verse many of the manifestations of double-mindedness are brought out: disobedience, compromise, rebellion, stubbornness, fear, and rejection. Saul epitomized double-mindedness. Because he never fully walked according to the ways of God, he also experienced divine rejection.

AHAB AND JEZEBEL

Another way we can see double-mindedness in action is by analyzing Ahab and Jezebel. These two individuals represent what God hates and are pictures of the two personalities within double-mindedness—rejection and rebellion.

> Ahab the son of Omri did more evil in the sight of the LORD than all who were before him...Ahab made an Asherah and did more to provoke the LORD God of Israel to anger than all the kings of Israel who preceded him.
> —1 KINGS 16:30, 33

Ahab was Israel's seventh king. He is known for promoting the worship of Baal and Ashtoreth and temple prostitution, in which men and women volunteered to serve as prostitutes in order to raise money for religious activities. He is also known for having occasional bouts of righteousness but then being quickly led away from God by the influence of his manipulative, heathen wife, Jezebel.

> The sins of Jeroboam the son of Nebat were seen as minor for him to walk in, for he took Jezebel the daughter of Ethbaal, king of the Sidonians, as his wife and went and served Baal and worshipped him.
> —1 KINGS 16:31

During the reign of Ahab and Jezebel, sexual rites of all kinds took place in God's temple—homosexuality, bestiality, and every disgraceful perversion you can think of. Women and men were worshipped for their physical beauty. The display of sexual organs was widespread.

> For they also built them high places and images, and
> groves, on every high hill, and under every green tree.
>   —1 Kings 14:23, kjv

The word *groves*, as used in the verse above, is found in the
King James Version of the Bible seventeen times. Fifteen of
those references refer to Ashtoreth and idolatrous temple worship. These "services" were held outside in the groves of trees
near the temple, where huge carvings of both male and female
sexual organs were displayed and worshipped.[3]

This is what Ahab allowed to come into Israel through Jezebel.
Lust and perversion are part of the rejection personality.

Ahab is a picture of the inward manifestation of double-
mindedness (rejection). Ahab is full of fear, sexual lust, insecurity, self-pity, fantasy, depression, jealousy, envy, hopelessness,
guilt, shame, and pouting.

Jezebel is a picture of the outward manifestation of double-
mindedness (rebellion). She was filled with stubbornness, self-
will, selfishness, confrontation, control, possessiveness, hatred,
resentment, murder, bitterness, witchcraft, and idolatry. See
here in 1 Kings 21:4–7 how these two fed into each other's
wickedness:

> Ahab returned home angry and depressed because of the
> answer Naboth the Jezreelite had given him, for he had
> said, "I will not give you the inheritance of my fathers."
> He lay down on his bed and sulked and would not eat
> any bread.
>
> But Jezebel his wife came to him and said, "Why is
> your spirit so sad that you refuse to eat bread?"
>
> And he said to her, "Because I spoke to Naboth the
> Jezreelite and said to him, 'Give me your vineyard for

money; or else, if you prefer, I will give you another vine-yard for it.' And he answered, 'I will not give you my vineyard.'"

Jezebel his wife said to him, "Are you not the governor of the kingdom of Israel? Get up and eat bread, and let your heart be happy, for I will get the vineyard of Naboth the Jezreelite for you."

These two people worked together to advance wickedness in Israel. This is a picture of how the rejection and rebellion personalities work together and reinforce each other in the double-minded. These two personalities must be pulled apart and cast out. They both need to be destroyed within the double-minded person.

God judged Ahab and Jezebel and removed them both from Israel. They both brought much trouble and devastation to Israel. The northern tribes never recovered from this and were eventually swallowed up in Assyria. God, have mercy upon us and deliver us.

It is not uncommon to find both of these spirits working within an individual. They need each other and draw strength from each other. Jezebel could not do what she did without Ahab. Jezebel entered Israel through this marriage and brought Baal worship with her. Ahab also used Jezebel to do his dirty work. They worked together just like rejection and rebellion.

Ida Mae Hammond saw the double-minded bondage as two hands clenched together with the fingers joined together. These hands need to be pulled apart and the fingers separated in order to destroy this stronghold. They must be separated and cast out.[4]

STUCK BETWEEN TWO OPINIONS

Jezebel was domineering, manipulative, and seductive. She intimidated, threatened, lied, and did whatever it took to accomplish her end. She had Naboth killed in order to possess his vineyard for her husband. She also murdered the prophets of God and threatened Elijah's life. She was vengeful and vindictive. She was evil and wicked. There was no peace while Jezebel was active.

> When Joram saw Jehu he said, "Is it peace, Jehu?" And he said, "What peace, so long as the harlotries of your mother Jezebel and her sorceries are so many?"
>
> —2 KINGS 9:22

Rebellion is a wicked personality that needs to be renounced and cast out. Until we see how wicked it is, we will tolerate it and remain in bondage.

Ahab was lustful, weak, fearful, and tolerated wickedness. He allowed Jezebel to bring in the worship of Baal. He was passive and would not stand up for righteousness. This inward and withdrawn personality is also wicked and needs to be renounced and cast out. God hates it just as He hates rebellion. Rejection and rebellion are both demonic and hateful in God's eyes.

> Ahab said to Elijah, "Have you found me, my enemy?"
> And he answered, "I have found you, because you have sold yourself to work evil in the sight of the LORD. 'See, I will bring disaster upon you and will take away your posterity and will cut off all your males, both free and slave, who are left in Israel, and will make your house like the house of Jeroboam the son of Nebat and like the house of

> Baasha the son of Ahijah, for the provocation with which
> you have provoked Me to anger and made Israel to sin."'
> —1 KINGS 21:20–22

God judged Ahab and his house for his wickedness. God hates this personality because it is wicked. Ahab was idolatrous, compromising, lustful, covetous, and weak. He was a rejected man who was connected to a rebellious woman.

God judged Jezebel for her wickedness and caused dogs to eat her flesh. See her demise in 2 Kings 9. She was ruthless, murderous, treacherous, idolatrous, seductive, controlling, intimidating, and wicked. She was a rebellious woman who was full of witchcraft.

> Ahab men are double-minded compromisers. In 1 Kings chapter twenty, the powerful Syrian army twice came against Israel. Both times a prophet of God came to Ahab and told him that God was going to give a mighty miracle to Ahab and defeat the Syrians. God indeed routed the Syrians twice. Still, Ahab did not return to worshipping God. Yet, he inquired of God's prophets when he wanted help. (See 1 Kings 22:6.) Ahab men go to church if it is politically correct or for personal gain, not because they love God. They witness God's miracles and still refuse to give credit to the Lord.
>
> Jezebel is a witch by definition and action. Witchcraft is manipulation and control of others through demonic means. She seeks to control the minds of others through lies, complaining, threats, position, shame, pity, and whatever else she can use.[5]

ISRAEL HAD A SUCCESSION OF WEAK AND DOUBLE-MINDED LEADERS

And the head of Ephraim is Samaria, and the head of Samaria is the son of Remaliah. If you will not believe, surely you shall not be established.

Moreover the LORD spoke again to Ahaz, saying: Ask for a sign from the LORD your God. Make it either as deep as Sheol or as high as heaven.

But Ahaz said, I will not ask, nor will I tempt the LORD.

Then he said, "Hear now, O house of David. Is it a small thing for you to weary men, but will you weary my God also? Therefore the Lord Himself shall give you a sign: The virgin shall conceive, and bear a son, and shall call his name Immanuel.

—ISAIAH 7:9–14

Isaiah was a prophet to king Ahaz. He gave the word of the Lord to Ahaz, challenging him to ask for a sign. God wanted to assure Ahaz of His delivering power. Ahaz refused to ask. God would give him a sign. If he would not believe, he would not be established.

There is nothing worse than a double-minded, vacillating, wavering, compromising, and weak leader who refuses to believe. This was Ahaz's problem—double-mindedness.

At that time King Ahaz sent to the king of Assyria for help...And at the time that he was oppressed he increased in unfaithfulness against the LORD.

—2 CHRONICLES 28:16, 22

Ahaz sent to Assyria for help against his enemies—Syria and Israel's northern kingdom—instead of trusting God. This was even after being told by the prophet to ask for a sign. He was too double-minded to trust God.

Double-mindedness caused many of the kings to worship idols and form alliances with heathen nations.

> Most of the kings of Israel and Judah were double-minded in the scriptural sense recorded by James...Elder Bruce R. McConkie tersely but fully described a double-minded man in these words: "A fickle, wavering man, as contrasted with one who is constant and firm, who always sustains the cause of righteousness. A member of the Church who tries both to forsake and to follow the world and who does not serve the Lord with an eye single to his glory."[6]

Here are the kings of Israel and Judah who forsook the Law of God, worshipped idols, and brought sin and disgrace to the people of Israel:

Rehoboam (Judah)—Forsook the law of the Lord

Jeroboam (Israel)—Set up idols and false priesthood

Nadab (Israel)—Followed Jeroboam's pattern

Abijam (Judah)—"Walked in all the sins of his father" (1 Kings 15:3)

Baasha (Israel)—Followed the pattern of Jeroboam

Elah (Israel)—Was a drunkard—"made Israel to sin" (1 Kings 16:13)

Zimri (Israel)—Was a murderer and idolater (reigned seven days)

Omri (Israel)—Was a worse idolater than all before him

Ahab (Israel)—Was even worse than Omri; married Jezebel

What was the one cause of downfall? Was it not double-mindedness that led to disobedience? Did not Israel trust more in the world and work harder to obtain its rewards than they trusted in the Lord and worked to obtain His rewards?[7]

Both the kings of the Northern and Southern kingdoms also were double-minded.

God has provided us keys in His Word that point not only to who we are to be, but also to who we are not to be. God does not want us to waver and vacillate between love for Him and love for the world. He is a jealous God. He wants His people for Himself, to bless and prosper us in the path He has ordained. There is redemption, healing, and deliverance available from the sin of double-mindedness. The first thing we need to do is discover the entry point this demon uses. In the next chapter we will uncover the spirit of rejection, which is the devil's doorway to coming in and destroying the lives of God's people.

CHAPTER 4

THE DEVIL'S DOOR

The Spirit of Rejection

He was despised and rejected of men, a man of sorrows and acquainted with grief.

—Isaiah 53:3

HAVE BEEN MINISTERING deliverance for more than thirty years, and I am still amazed at the number of people who suffer from the spirit of rejection. The demonic spirit of double-mindedness first enters a person's life through rejection. The spirit of rejection is so common that it is always present in the demonized people to whom I minister. Rejection is a wound that usually begins early in life, and a wound left untreated develops into an infection. Demons are like germs that are attracted to a wound and cause an infection. In other words, what begins as a wound develops into something much worse.

Not only does rejection wound, but it also affects a person's identity. The person rejected feels as if there is something wrong with him, and therefore will reject himself. The spirit of self-rejection usually accompanies rejection. The enemy sets up false personalities within a person who has been rejected.

The core of the rejection personality is rejection, self-rejection, and fear of rejection. No one likes to be rejected. It is a hurtful and painful experience. Most people avoid it at all costs.

Fear is a stronghold within the rejection personality—fear of being rejected, hurt, laughed at, abandoned, mistreated, and so on. The rejection personality is the inward manifestation of double-mindedness, as we saw in Ahab, one of the kings of Israel. Rejection causes a person to withdraw or isolate oneself. This is a defense mechanism. It is the equivalent of the ostrich sticking its head in the sand.

Rejection is the sense of being unwanted, the agony of desperately wanting people to love you but being convinced they do not. They actually may be loving and accepting, but when you are suffering rejection you are unable to believe or receive it. There is an aching desire to be a part of something, but you never feel that you are.

Isaiah wrote about a woman who had suffered a deep and terrible spiritual wound because of rejection:

For the LORD has called you as a woman forsaken and grieved in spirit, and a wife of youth when you were refused, says your God.

—ISAIAH 54:6

To compensate for rejection some become withdrawn like a turtle in his shell for protection. Others explode with anger and hatred, fighting bitterly against the pain and injustice. Rejected people often spend their lives seeking a meaningful identity outside of a true relationship with God.[1]

How Rejection Enters

Rejection often begins at a young age; it can even start in the womb. Prenatal rejection is common and can occur with unplanned/accidental pregnancies; traumatic or stressful labor; attempted abortion; pregnancy problems; an unwanted child; illegitimacy; rejection from the father, mother, or both; and rape.

Another form of prenatal rejection occurs when the parents desperately want to have a child of a specific gender but find out that their child will be of the opposite gender. All their prayers and hopes are focused toward having a child of a certain gender. But when the child is born of the opposite gender, it is rejected or abandoned. This is common in certain cultures where one gender is given privilege and status over the other.

In your own experiences you may have seen instances where a father wanted a son but had a girl instead, yet he tries to interact with her as if she were his son by pushing her to participate in certain activities, wear certain clothes, or behave in uncharacteristic ways. The same thing can happen with mothers who wanted a girl but ended up birthing a boy. Other deliverance ministers have pointed out that this could be the root of the gender issues many gay, lesbian, bisexual, and transgender individuals deal with.

A person can also be rejected by his or her family. This kind of rejection can include abandonment by one or both parents, whether intentional or perceived; emotional or physical abuse from authority figures; adopted children; children with birth defects; birth order (middle child syndrome; middle children can be vulnerable if they feel the parents favor the elder or younger children); favoritism among children; death of a parent; parental neglect; overbearing parents; or a perfectionist parent.

Societal rejection includes rejection from peers due to awkward features, racial prejudice, social and economic differences, bullying, and mistreatment from authority figures (i.e., teachers or coaches).

Causes of rejection at the beginning of life:

- Being born with the gender opposite what the parents wanted
- Being born with a deformity or physical disability
- Constant criticism by parents, siblings, or authority figures
- Unjust discipline, particularly if another family member appears to be favored
- Being called names that emphasize embarrassing personal features

- A sick or incapacitated brother or sister receiving prolonged medical care and attention

- Fathers showing weakness, apathy, or passivity in their authority or responsibility roles

- Subjection to sexual molestation or incest

- A father becoming sexually aggressive to his wife in the presence of his children

- Spoiling or pampering a child

- Children who belong to a racial minority will usually feel rejected by the majority amongst whom they live and play

- Speech difficulties such as stuttering, stammering, lisping, or an inability to pronounce certain consonants or words

- Unhappy parents who argue, fight, won't talk to each other, or only speak to their children—the children will feel guilty and responsible

- Parental cruelty

- Alcoholism in one or both parents

- Failure to be forgiven or trusted by the parents

- Bribes or threats to be academically successful

- Being expelled from school or rejected by a peer group

- Being embarrassed over the parents' religious beliefs

- A father showing more attention to his daughter's girlfriends than he does to his own daughter

- Destruction of the family home by fire or some natural disaster

- A family member convicted of a serious crime

- A sudden drop in the family's standard of living caused by the unemployment, redundancy, or bankruptcy of the breadwinner

- Parents who have ample financial resources but show meanness toward their children, causing them to feel ashamed before their playmates

- Children constantly being left to their own resources either because of the working hours of their parents or disinterest in their children's welfare

- Parents showing no active interest in the progress of their children's schoolwork, sports activities, or leisure time pursuits

Causes of rejection later in life:

- Being deserted or divorced by a mate

- Experiencing the death or unfaithfulness of a marriage partner

- Mental or physical cruelty caused by a husband or wife

- Shame caused by a court conviction of a criminal offense

- Having to serve a prison term

- Inability to find any long-term relief for mental, emotional, or physical problems after having exhausted all forms of counseling or professional services

- Incompatible religious ideologies in marriage causing one partner to be forced to comply with the other's wishes

- A lowering of lifestyle standards caused by drug or alcohol addictions of a marriage partner

- Rejection in love or a broken engagement

- Becoming bedridden or crippled as a result of disease or an accident

- Becoming subject to pressures beyond one's ability to control

- Being fired from a place of employment for incompetency or being unable to find employment over a long period of time

- Being totally let down by people who had been trusted and whose advice had been totally relied upon

- Financial embarrassment caused by the failure of investments taken on by the advice of a close friend or being financially cheated by unscrupulous operators

DEMONIC SPIRITS ASSOCIATED WITH REJECTION

Rejection is not only a demon, but it is also a personality. The rejection personality is comprised of different spirits that join rejection and strengthen rejection. Demons are like gangs. Just as different gangs have different personalities, the same is true when demons gang up in an individual. Demons are drawn to emotional pain and will come into a person suffering from rejection. Demonic spirits that come in as a result of rejection include the following:

Lust

Lust is a demonic substitute for true love. Rejected people will seek out relationships and often get involved in sexual immorality at a young age. The spirit of harlotry can manifest at a young age and can be seen in young women who dress provocatively.

Sexual impurity has become rampant in our society. Sexual lust spirits include adultery, fornication, whoredom, harlotry, seduction, sexual impurity, perversion, homosexuality, lesbianism, masturbation, pornography, incest, fantasy lust, sodomy, and uncleanness.

Lust is not only sexual but can also manifest in materialism, overindulgence, food addictions (gluttony, bulimia, anorexia, and extreme dieting), drug and alcohol addictions, clothing, and so on.

Fantasy

The fantasy cluster of demons includes pornography and daydreaming, and can lead to having excessive hobbies into which the person can flee to escape reality.

Perversion

The perversion cluster of demons can lead to homosexuality, lesbianism, fetishes, molestation, and other deviant sexual activities. Perversion can be a manifestation of self-rejection when people reject their own sexual identity. These are simply attempts to overcome rejection.

Insecurity and inferiority

Rejection makes a person feel low and causes low self-esteem.

Pride, vanity, and ego

These three manifestations are compensation spirits for rejection. These spirits attempt to make people feel better about themselves.

Self-accusation

This occurs when the person blames himself or herself for the rejection. "Is there something wrong with me? Maybe I am not good enough. Maybe it's my fault."

Depression

This manifestation includes despondency, despair, discouragement, and hopelessness. There are multitudes of people who suffer from bouts of depression. Many of them are being medicated. Going in and out of depression is a sign of double-mindedness. This also includes withdrawal and isolation. Depression is at an all-time high. There are many people being treated for manic depression (bipolar disorder). This can even drive people to hopelessness and suicide. Depression can cause a person to desire to escape, which can lead to sleepiness and abusing alcohol and drugs.

Perfectionism

When a person has suffered rejection, he will tend to attempt to compensate by doing everything perfectly hoping that no one will reject him. This becomes bondage and opens the door to spirits of pride, ego, and vanity. Some of the signs of the perfectionism spirits include obsessive-compulsive behavior; rechecking the work of others; having legalistic, religious, or Pharisee spirits; and being nitpicky, critical, judgmental, intolerant, frustrated, and hypocritical. People with the spirit of perfectionism will force others to reject them, driving the rejection deeper, because they are almost impossible to live with.

Parents who have the spirit of perfectionism can be intolerant and overbearing on their children; husbands or wives can be intolerant toward mates; pastors can be intolerant toward members; and so on. Perfectionistic people are intolerant of those who do not meet their standard of perfection.

Perfectionism also leads to legalism and religious spirits. The perfectionist hides behind the rule book, and makes the Bible a rule book. This leads to hypocrisy and covering up because the perfectionist cannot admit he or she has broken the rules.

Deliverance is needed so the person can walk in love, compassion, and mercy toward others. Remember, perfectionism is rooted in rejection; the person seeking deliverance must fall out of agreement with the rejection personality and allow the Lord to develop his or her real personality.

Unfairness

The rejected person often feels that life is unfair and people are unfair. They will often take up causes to rid the world of unfairness. This is a manifestation of false compassion and false responsibility. They often get involved in animal rights, environmental rights, homosexual rights, and the like. Sometimes these groups become violent in their attempts to rid the world of unfairness. Anger, bitterness, rebellion, and resentment are the opposite strongholds of unfairness and rejection. There is a biblical gift of mercy that has true compassion on the hurting, but false compassion is fleshly and demonic.

Guilt, shame, and confusion

This cluster of demons includes condemnation, unworthiness, and shame. Shame is defined as a painful emotion caused by a strong sense of guilt, embarrassment, unworthiness, or disgrace. Shame is connected to confusion: "My confusion is continually before me, and the shame of my face hath covered me" (Ps. 44:15, KJV).

Sensitiveness

Rejected people are easily hurt or damaged and are delicately aware of the attitudes and feelings of others. Rejected people are overly sensitive to every word and action. They are easily offended.

Inordinate affection for animals

Rejected people desire love and will receive the unconditional love of a pet. There is nothing wrong with having affection for pets as long as it is not inordinate.

Fear

Fear includes the fears of abandonment, failure, hurt, rejection, dying, witchcraft, authority, germs, darkness, marriage, dogs, accidents, man, Jezebel, confrontation, poverty, and more. There are also extreme fears such as panic, panic attacks, terror, apprehension, sudden fear, and more. Talkativeness, nervousness, worry, anxiety, and tension can also be part of the fear cluster of demons related to rejection.

Paranoia

Paranoia, as we saw demonstrated in King Saul, is defined as a tendency on the part of an individual or group toward excessive or irrational suspiciousness; distrust of others that is not based on objective reality but on a need to defend the ego against unconscious impulses that use projection as a mechanism of defense and that often takes the form of compensatory megalomania. Megalomania is an obsession with grandiose or extravagant things or actions.[2] Those who are obsessed with power, fame, and status can often be paranoid, believing everyone is out to take from them.

Paranoia can be seen in blaming others, accusation, delusional accusation, and suspicion, and is rooted in fear. Paranoia is the baseless suspicion of the motives of others. It is rooted in fear and rejection. The rejection personality always questions the motives of others and judges them without a cause.

Indecision

We talked about this one in chapter 2, but to put it in its proper place and discuss it in the context of rejection is important. Indecision results in procrastination, compromise, confusion, forgetfulness, and indifference. Indecision is one of the most debilitating problems in life because life is based on decisions. Indifference is an attitude that causes a person to avoid making decisions.

Passivity

Passivity causes listlessness and lethargy, continual sadness, crying, defeatism, dejection, despair, despondency, discouragement, escapism, fatigue, gloom, gluttony, grief, guilt, heartache, heartbreak, hopelessness, hurt, hyperactivity, indifference, inner hurts, insomnia, laziness, lethargy, listlessness, loneliness, mourning, negativity, passivity, rejection, self-pity, sorrow, and tiredness. Many times, a person fighting passivity will feel like he is in a "funk," like he is going nowhere.

I have often taught on the danger of passivity. Passivity immobilizes a person and results in withdrawal and lethargy. It takes away the natural desire to be aggressive in life. Passive people will not pursue and go after what they need to succeed in life. Passive people will let others do it for them.

REJECTION AND THE CRIMINAL MIND

In the past I've done teachings on "criminal schizophrenia" in my series on double-mindedness. People with a history of criminal activity are usually in need of deliverance from double-mindedness. The rebellion personality in the double-minded includes spirits of bitterness, violence, murder, retaliation, lawlessness, and antisubmissiveness. These spirits are also connected to rejection.

Persons who have been incarcerated for criminal activity (especially violent crimes) will need deliverance after being released, and the church is often ill-equipped to minister to these individuals because of the lack of deliverance and the lack of revelation in the area of double-mindedness.

In those who are or have been incarcerated, rejection is compounded by social rejection. Convicted felons have a difficult time once they are released back into society. They also have a difficult time staying faithful to Christ because of double-mindedness, which will often cause them to go back into criminal activity. They need acceptance, love, and deliverance from those who understand the schizophrenic revelation uncovered by Frank and Ida Mae Hammond, and understand how rejection and rebellion work to hinder a person from becoming stable in his or her personality.

REJECTION MUST GO!

We have all been rejected in one way or another. According to deliverance ministers Noel and Phyl Gibson:

> Having prayed for believers of many nations, I have come to this conclusion: the greatest undiagnosed, therefore, untreated malady in the body of Christ today is rejection. Rejection, whether active or passive, real or imaginary, robs Jesus Christ of His rightful lordship in the life of His children and robs them of the vitality and quality of life that Jesus intended.[3]

We must be able to identify the causes of rejection and come against the demons of rejection, fear of rejection, self-rejection, hereditary rejection, roots of rejection, and the spirits that come in with rejection: hurt, anger, bitterness, rage, pride, fear, rebellion, and more. All of these things can torment your life. Jesus does not want you to be tormented. He wants you to be set free. You are not alone. So many people need deliverance from these demons of rejection and the other demons that accompany the demons of rejection. God wants to set us all free from the spirit of rejection so that we can bring deliverance to our families and friends and those around us.

CHAPTER 5

AS THE SIN OF WITCHCRAFT

The Spirit of Rebellion

*For rebellion is as the sin of witchcraft, and stubbornness is
as iniquity and idolatry. Because you have rejected the word
of the LORD, He has also rejected you from being king.*

—1 SAMUEL 15:23

REBELLION IS THE other of the two personalities of double-mindedness. It often comes into a person's life as a result of rejection. When you examine the behavior of a young child, you will notice that rebellion is often a cry for attention. The core of the rebellion personality is rebellion, disobedience, and antisubmissiveness. The rebellion personality is the outward personality; it is the polar opposite of the rejection personality, which is inward. The rebellion personality acts out, lashes out, and shows out.

Samuel rebuked King Saul for his rebellion by equating it with witchcraft, as you read in the opening verse of this chapter.

Demonic Spirits Associated With Rebellion

Rebellion is a cluster of demons in the double-minded personality that comes with many other related spirits. Here is a list of related spirits that need to be cast out.

Stubbornness

Stubbornness is being stiff-necked and refusing to submit to a yoke. This manifestation of rebellion shows up as antisubmissiveness, unteachableness, and idolatry (1 Sam. 15:23). Stubborn people are oftentimes unable to receive ministry, hear correction, as they always think they are right. Stubbornness is also connected to drunkenness and gluttony:

> They shall say to the elders of his city, "This son of ours is stubborn and rebellious. He will not listen to us. He is a glutton and a drunkard."
> —Deuteronomy 21:20

Stubbornness keeps you from being steadfast:

> And they might not be as their fathers, a stubborn and
> rebellious generation, a generation that did not set their
> heart steadfast, and whose spirit was not faithful to God.
> —PSALM 78:8

As I discussed earlier, Israel was stubborn. Israel was also double-minded. *Stubborn* is the Hebrew word *carar*, meaning backsliding, rebellious, revolter/revolting, slide back. Double-mindedness is the root cause of backsliding. Israel was stiff necked and resistant to the Holy Spirit.

> You stiff-necked people, uncircumcised in heart and ears!
> You always resist the Holy Spirit. As your fathers did, so
> do you.
> —ACTS 7:51

Stubbornness can block the flow of the Holy Spirit. Those who are stubborn will not submit to God or His Spirit. They will reject the word of the Lord. Many reject present truth being spoken today because of stubbornness. Change is a part of life. You cannot grow without change. We must be flexible in order to change with God. There are always new things being birthed and released in the kingdom.

Israel was often referred to as a "stiff-necked people" (Exod. 33:3). The term *stiff-necked* is a reference to stubbornness. Stephen called those who resist the Holy Ghost "stiff-necked" and "uncircumcised in heart" (Acts 7:51). Deuteronomy 31:27 says, "For I know your rebellion and your stiff neck." The Moffatt translation says, "For I know your defiant temper and your stubborn spirit." Stubbornness is a refusal to repent and turn from the crooked way.

Psalm 75:5 says, "Do not lift up your horn on high; do not speak with a stiff neck" (NKJV). To lift up the horn means to boast or to flaunt power. It means to be arrogant and irreverent. It means to defy God (defiance). This is associated with a stiff neck. Refusal to hear, antisubmissiveness, and unteachableness are all tied in with being stiff-necked (Jer. 17:23). These are also manifestations of pride and Leviathan.

Another characteristic of this spirit is being unyielding and unbending (Job 41:23). To yield means to submit by giving way before force, argument, persuasion, or entreaty. It means to relinquish one's rights. People who are "set in their ways" (unbending and unyielding) are being controlled by rebellion and pride. They refuse to yield.

Many believers suffer from hardness of heart just as the disciples did. Pharaoh hardened his heart and was destroyed in the Red Sea. Hardness of heart, which comes alongside stubbornness, prevents us from walking in the fullness of God's blessings.

Delusion

People bound by a spirit of delusion deceive themselves into believing they are someone they are not. This is a false personality. Some people try to overcome rejection by thinking themselves to be some great person—singer, actor, lover, preacher, and the like. The spirit of delusion comes along and says, "You are really somebody. You are a spiritual [or some other kind of] giant!" Delusion includes self-deception, self-delusion, and self-seduction.

Selfishness

To be selfish is to be concerned chiefly or only with oneself. King Saul became preoccupied with himself and his kingdom. He became very selfish and was preoccupied with preserving his rule. The narcissistic spirit is manifested through extreme self-centeredness. (Narcissus, a person in Greek mythology known for his beauty, fell in love with his own reflection in the water of a spring.)

Witchcraft

This spirit manifests in different ways, including sorcery, divination, intimidation, control, and manipulation. Saul, a biblical example of rebellion and double-mindedness, consulted with the witch of Endor:

> Then said Saul to his servants, "Seek for me a woman who is a medium, that I may go to her and inquire of her." And his servants said to him, "There is woman medium in Endor."
>
> —1 Samuel 28:7

He also manifested the spirit of witchcraft when he plotted to trap David and take his life through manipulation and deceit:

> And Saul commanded his servants, saying, "Speak to David in secret saying, 'Listen, the king delights in you and all his servants love you. Now therefore become the king's son-in-law.'"
>
> —1 Samuel 18:22

Saul then turned on his own son Jonathan, who was defending David. He accused Jonathan of choosing David over him. This is another characteristic of the rebellion personality—accusation.

> Then Saul was angry with Jonathan and he said to him,
> "You son of a perverse rebellious woman, do I not know
> that you are choosing the son of Jesse to your own shame,
> and to the shame of your mother's nakedness?"
>
> —1 Samuel 20:30

Jezebel is another classic example of a person using witchcraft to gain what one desires:

> When Joram saw Jehu he said, "Is it peace, Jehu?" And
> he said, "What peace, so long as the harlotries of your
> mother Jezebel and her sorceries are so many?"
>
> —2 Kings 9:22

> The demon of witchcraft can also work in many other
> kinds of relationships. A pastor may seek to control
> members of his staff or his entire congregation. A business executive may intimidate his subordinates....People
> who habitually use manipulation or intimidation to control others open themselves to the bondage and influence
> of a demon of witchcraft. If this happens, they will be
> unable to relate to anyone apart from these tactics. It will
> be no longer just the flesh at work, but a supernatural
> power that can bring whomever they control into a condition of spiritual slavery.[1]

The whole realm of the occult falls under the umbrella of witchcraft. This includes false religions, fortune-telling, New Age, ESP, astrology, hypnosis, Eastern religions, masonry, telepathy, palmistry, etc. These are all manifestations of rebellion. Double-minded people are usually attracted to the occult.

Control and possessiveness

To control is to exercise authoritative or dominating influence over; direct.[2]

> Controlling people work hard to manipulate other people, events, and circumstances to make things go their way. They spend their waking hours trying to figure out how to spin, engineer, and manipulate situations to their advantage and gain. These people get very upset and angry when things don't go their way. They convince themselves that the world around them will fall apart if they are not in control, whether it is at home or at work or where ever they are in what every position or situation they are in. They must be in control to be comfortable. They think that nothing can be done right; nothing can happen that is any good without them, without their input, without their direction and control.[3]

Possessiveness is "having or manifesting a desire to control or dominate another, especially in order to limit that person's relationships with others...an excessive desire to possess, control, or dominate."[4] This can be seen in individual relationships, and even in relationships between leaders and followers.

Bitterness

The core of the rebellion personality is the root of bitterness (Heb. 12:15). I will spend more time on this spirit in the next chapter because it is such a significant stronghold in the rebellion personality and causes many people to have difficulty finding deliverance from double-mindedness.

A person can develop a root of bitterness from the hurt and pain of rejection. The root of bitterness has related spirits, including unforgiveness, rage, anger, violence, revenge, retaliation, and even murder. The Hebrew word for bitterness, *marah*, connects bitterness and rebellion. *Marah* means "to be (causatively, make) bitter (or unpleasant); (figuratively) to rebel (or resist, cause to provoke)—bitter change, be disobedient, disobey, grievously, provocation, provoke(-ing), (be) rebel (against, -lious)."[5] Bitterness is repressed anger and is connected to stubbornness (refusal to forgive).

The rejected person often has a hard time forgiving. Rejection hurts and creates offense, which requires forgiveness. Unforgiveness can breed bitterness. The double-minded person often vividly remembers the hurts of the past. They sometimes have a problem with memory recall. The continual memory of past offenses keeps alive unforgiveness, bitterness, and hatred. (See Acts 8:23; Romans 3:14; Ephesians 4:31; 1 Samuel 18:11–12.)

Bitterness is a destructive spirit that can ruin a person's life from the inside out.

Strife

The double-minded person is always in a storm in relationships. Because strife includes contention, fighting, arguing, bickering, quarreling, and the like, there are many broken relationships that are the result of double-mindedness.

DANGERS OF REBELLION

Rebellion will get you into serious trouble and bondage. Obedience and humility will bring great blessing to your life. Beware of disobedience and rebellion, and repent and receive deliverance if needed. Here are some of the dangers of rebellion:

Rebellion is equated with witchcraft. (See 1 Samuel 15:23.)

Rebellion can cause you to dwell in a dry land.

> God sets the deserted in families; He brings out prisoners
> into prosperity, but the *rebellious* dwell in a dry land.
> —PSALM 68:6, EMPHASIS ADDED

Rebellion can cause you to dwell in darkness and the shadow
of death, bound in affliction and iron.

> Some sit in darkness and in the shadow of death, being
> prisoners in affliction and irons, because they *rebelled*
> against the words of God and rejected the counsel of the
> Most High. Therefore He brought down their hearts with
> hard labor; they fell down, and there was none to help.
> —PSALM 107:10–12, EMPHASIS ADDED

Rebellion can cause to you be devoured by the sword (death).

> But if you refuse and *rebel*, you shall be devoured with
> the sword; for the mouth of the LORD has spoken it.
> —ISAIAH 1:20, EMPHASIS ADDED

Rebellion can make you an enemy of God.

> But they *rebelled* and grieved His Holy Spirit; therefore,
> He turned Himself to be their enemy, and He fought
> against them.
> —ISAIAH 63:10, EMPHASIS ADDED

Rebellion can bring sorrow and captivity.

> The LORD is in the right, for I have *rebelled* against
> His commandment. Hear now, all peoples, and see my

sorrow; my virgins and my young men have gone into captivity.
—LAMENTATIONS 1:18, EMPHASIS ADDED

Rebellion can cause you distress and cause your bowels (emotions) to be troubled.

Look, O LORD, for I am in distress; my soul is greatly troubled; my heart is overturned within me, for I have grievously *rebelled*. In the street the sword bereaves, at home it is like death.
—LAMENTATIONS 1:20, EMPHASIS ADDED

God can and will forgive rebellion, and you can receive His mercy.

To the Lord our God belong mercies and forgiveness, though we have rebelled against Him.
—DANIEL 9:9, EMPHASIS ADDED

Rebellion causes us to have hard hearts. God can't work with us when our hearts are hard. That is why in Ezekiel 36:26–30, God said:

Also, I will give you a new heart, and a new spirit I will put within you. And I will take away the stony heart out of your flesh, and I will give you a heart of flesh. I will put My Spirit within you and cause you to walk in My statutes, and you will keep My judgments and do them. You will dwell in the land that I gave to your fathers. And you will be My people, and I will be your God. I will also save you from all your uncleanness. And I will call for the grain and increase it and lay no famine upon you. I will multiply the fruit of the tree and the increase of the field so that you shall receive no more reproach of famine among the nations.

God desires to bless us, to multiply and increase our fields, so that we are no longer a reproach. Part of His redemption plan is to bring us into a good place and cause us to live fruitful and productive lives. This cannot be sustained while we are bitter, rebellious, prideful, and hard-hearted. But through deliverance we are transformed, healed, and restored to a place in which God can begin to build us up.

CHAPTER 6

THAT WHICH DEFILES

The Root of Bitterness

Watching diligently so that no one falls short of the grace of God, lest any root of bitterness spring up to cause trouble, and many become defiled by it.

—HEBREWS 12:15

T HE CORE OF the rebellion personality is the root of bitterness. A person can develop a root of bitterness from the hurt and pain of rejection. The root of bitterness has related spirits including unforgiveness, resentment, rage, anger, violence, revenge, retaliation, and even murder.

As I mentioned before, the Hebrew word for bitterness is *marah*, which means "to be (causatively, make) bitter (or unpleasant); (figuratively) to rebel (or resist, cause to provoke)— bitter change, be disobedient, disobey, grievously, provocation, provoke(-ing), (be) rebel (against, -lious)."[1] I will expound more on the significance of *marah* in the next chapter.

By examining the various shades of meaning, it is obvious that rebellion and bitterness have the same root. It is commonly said that if you stay rebellious, you will become bitter, and if you stay bitter, you will become rebellious. When dealing with someone who is rebellious, you will often find that they have or will become bitter. Bitterness is also connected to rejection. When someone has been rejected, they often rebel and take on a root of bitterness. And because rejection hurts so badly, many people become unforgiving, resentful, and bitter.

One of the major desires of Satan is that we become rebellious; if we are disobedient and rebellious against God and His Word, then our lives are opened up for destruction. The Bible says, "If you are willing and obedient, you shall eat the good of the land; but if you refuse and rebel, you shall be devoured with the sword; for the mouth of the LORD has spoken it." (Isa. 1:19–20).

Rebellion is a very destructive force or demon in a person's life. If you want to obey God, if you want to be submitted to God, if you want the blessing of the Lord upon your life, be "willing and obedient" and "you shall eat the good of the land."

I was listening to the news one day, and I heard poor people on the program railing against the rich. The only problem with that is the fact that most poor people want to be rich. Everybody wants the blessing of God, and when they don't have it they talk about the ones who do. People want to be blessed. No one wants to live their life cursed. No one wants to struggle. No one wants to be defeated. No one wants to be the tail. No one wants to be last. No one wants to suffer. No one wants to be down. Everybody wants the blessing of the Lord on their lives. People want God's blessing. They want to know what they can do to be blessed. Well, Isaiah 1:19 tells us, "If you are willing and obedient, you shall eat the good of the land."

The blessing of God always comes from obeying His voice, so one of the ways to not be blessed is to be disobedient, rebellious, and hard-hearted. If we operate in rebellion against the Word of God and the plan of God, and go opposite the way that God says to go, then of course God's blessing will not come upon our lives. So we definitely do not want anything in our lives to make us bitter, because bitterness is one of the root conditions of rebellion.

The Bible says in the Book of Exodus, chapter 1, that the Egyptians made the people of Israel's lives bitter through hard bondage (Exod. 1:13–14). You can become bitter just by going through so much in life. You can become angry and bitter at God, blaming Him and questioning, "Why is my life so hard? Why am I having so much difficulty in my life? Why am I struggling so much?" Abuse, mistreatment, rape, molestation, abandonment, being taken advantage of, rejection, hurt, broken-heartedness, sadness, and sorrow can cause you to be bitter.

There are so many different ways life can deal you a bitter hand. You have to guard your heart, because out of it flows the issues of life. You cannot allow your heart to become bitter or unforgiving. If you allow unforgiveness and bitterness to get into your heart, you will be open to rebellion and will not walk in the blessing of God. So it is very important that we guard ourselves from unforgiveness, resentment, bitterness, anger, hatred, revenge, retaliation, and other such things. No matter what has happened to us, when we release things and forgive people we are also able to receive deliverance so we can really walk in healing, health, prosperity, favor, and the blessing of God.

We've dealt with many people in deliverance ministry with such spirits. Sometimes these spirits are repressed, hidden, and not easily seen. With some people, when they talk to you, you can hear that they are bitter. But there are also those whose bitterness is hidden. You would not even suspect them of being bitter at all. This is why it is called a "root of bitterness" in Hebrews 12:15: "[Be careful] lest any root of bitterness spring up to cause trouble, and many become defiled by it." A root is something that is underground. You can't see it. A root feeds the tree. The tree produces fruit, but you cannot see roots. They are the life source of a tree or plant. So if you want to destroy the fruit, you have to cut the root system.

> Even now the axe is put to the tree roots. Therefore, every tree which does not bear good fruit is cut down and thrown into the fire.
> —MATTHEW 3:10

GETTING TO THE ROOT

In addition to the obvious players of rejection and rebellion, bitterness is also a result of repressed anger and is connected to stubbornness (refusal to forgive). The rejected (and therefore, rebellious) person often has a hard time forgiving. Rejection hurts and creates offense, which requires forgiveness. The double-minded person often remembers the hurts of the past vividly. They sometimes have a problem with memory recall. The continual memory of past offenses keeps alive unforgiveness, bitterness, and hatred.

We can also find how bitterness is connected to sorcery through the story of Simon the sorcerer, specifically in Acts 8:23, right after the apostle Peter calls Simon out for not having the right heart in seeking after the power of the Holy Spirit: "For I see that you are in the gall of bitterness," Peter says, "and in the bond of iniquity." Something in Simon's life left him bitter and caused him to be open to the spirit of witchcraft, which I pointed out in the previous chapter is directly connected to rebellion. Simon the sorcerer, like Jezebel, was operating under the spirit of rebellion.

Bitterness is also exposed through cursing, angry outbursts, and malice:

> Their mouths are full of cursing and bitterness.
>
> —ROMANS 3:14

> Let all bitterness, wrath, anger, outbursts, and blasphemies, with all malice, be taken away from you.
>
> —EPHESIANS 4:31

Bitterness can produce rage and murder, as the Bible reveals through the story of Saul and David. In one instance, Saul's bitterness was manifested through rage and murder when he threw a javelin at David:

And Saul threw the spear. For he said, "I will pin David to the wall." But David avoided him two times. Saul was afraid of David because the LORD was with him but had departed from Saul.

—1 SAMUEL 18:11–12

The root of bitterness shows itself through the following:

- Anger
- Unforgiveness
- Hatred
- Revenge
- Violence
- Arguing
- Wrath
- Strife
- Murder
- Retaliation
- Temper
- Contention

Bitterness is a root, thereby making it harder to identify and expose than many surface issues, but nonetheless it's a deadly poison that needs to be released. If left alone, it will grow and fester, and it has the ability to spring up many surface issues such as irritability, anger, hatred, etc. Individuals who have a root of bitterness will often find it easy to become upset over little things that go on around them. It is easy for them to look at the circumstances around them as the source of their problems, rather than seeing how they are handling those circumstances. Instead of letting it go and forgiving, they let it get to them, and it devours them alive. This is a very common route by which demons enter people today.[2]

What the Bible Teaches About the Demon of Bitterness

When I am teaching on the subject of deliverance, I sometimes prefer to use the word *demon* instead of *spirit* because *demon* says what it really is—a demon. There needs to be no doubt that we are dealing with demons. In the Bible, Jesus says, "In My name they will cast out demons" (Mark 16:17). In the King James Version the word is "devils." The words *demon* and *devil* are interchangeable. The demon of bitterness needs to be cast out of our lives. The first step in doing this is calling it out for what it is: bitterness is a demon that wreaks havoc on people's lives and keeps them from experiencing the full blessing of a covenant with God. In this section I am going to take you through the Bible to help you fully understand how this demonic power works against the believer.

If you look up the words *bitter* and *bitterness* in a Bible concordance, find the first time the word or words are mentioned in the Bible, and begin to read and study from that first reference, you are practicing what is called the law of first reference or the law of first mention. This is "the principle that requires one to go to that portion of the Scriptures where a doctrine is mentioned for the first time and to study the first occurrence of the same in order to get the fundamental inherent meaning of that doctrine."[3] Often the Spirit of God will use that first reference to give you a revelation of the particular subject. This is what I will walk you through as we learn more about this demon.

How bitterness enters

The first time the word *bitter* is mentioned in the Bible is Genesis 27:34, in connection with Esau. But if we study this verse in the context of the surrounding text, we see how bitterness first enters into someone's life:

> When Esau heard the words of his father, he cried with a great and exceedingly bitter cry, and said to his father, "Bless me, even me also, O my father!"
>
> He said, "Your brother came deceitfully and has taken away your blessing."
>
> Esau said, "Is he not rightly named Jacob? For he has supplanted me these two times. He took away my birthright, and now he has taken away my blessing." And he said, "Have you not reserved a blessing for me?"
>
> Then Isaac answered and said to Esau, "I have made him your lord, and I have given to him all his brothers as servants; and I have sustained him with grain and new wine. What can I now do for you, my son?"
>
> And Esau said to his father, "Do you have only one blessing, my father? Bless me, even me also, O my father!" Then Esau lifted up his voice and wept.
>
> Isaac his father answered and said to him, "Your dwelling shall be away from the fatness of the earth and away from the dew of heaven from above. You will live by your sword and will serve your brother. When you become restless, you will break his yoke from your neck."
>
> So Esau hated Jacob because of the blessing with which his father blessed him. And Esau said in his heart, "The days of mourning for my father are at hand; then I will kill my brother Jacob."
>
> —Genesis 27:34–41

This passage reveals the first way bitterness comes into a person's life. When something that belongs to a person is unlawfully stolen or taken away, he feels that someone has taken from his life the honor or blessing that rightfully belonged to him, or that someone has cheated him out of something. This is especially hard for men. That position, blessing, those finances—whatever it is—should have been his. He believes that something rightfully belonged to him, but somehow a "Jacob"—an individual who robs and steals what rightfully belongs to someone else—came in and cheated him out of what was his.

Esau should have received the blessing because he was the firstborn, but his brother, Jacob, pretended to be Esau and stole his blessing. Once that blessing was given, it could not be taken back. This caused Esau to be bitter.

We all have come across people who feel like they have been cheated out of something. There are so many who feel as though they got a raw deal out of life. They didn't get the job or promotion. They didn't get the blessing they hoped for, the spouse they prayed for, and on and on. Now they are bitter and angry. Some are so upset about it that they want to harm or kill the person they see as responsible for what they didn't get. They feel that the circumstances surrounding their loss are completely unfair: "I was robbed, I was cheated, someone lied, and I did not receive what was rightfully mine." This is how Satan brings the demon of bitterness into a person's life.

The only way to keep your heart clear of bitterness is to walk in love and forgiveness. But when you are in the flesh—and Esau represents the flesh—you will always respond according to the flesh through anger, hatred, and murder. If you were in the Spirit, you would not respond with bitterness. That is not the way the Spirit responds.

As I said, Esau represents the flesh. His name means "hairy" and "rough."[4] Hebrews 12:16 calls Esau "profane." This means he was debase, disrespectful, irreverent, and vulgar. In essence he was ungodly, worldly, fleshly, and carnal. His reaction demonstrates how the flesh reacts when it feels it has been wronged. The flesh always opens the door for bitterness, anger, hatred, and murder. We see all of these demons manifested in the verses above.

Before we are saved, every one of us is in the flesh. We don't have the Spirit of God dwelling in us yet, who helps overcome the hurtful and evil things people do. Life is full of people who mistreat others and steal from them. That's life. There will always be someone trying to get ahead of you by taking what's yours and getting it for themselves. Satan will try to destroy you through the actions of other people. All of us have to deal with this fact in life. Yes, there are some things that rightfully belonged to you. You earned or had favor for the blessings, position, promotion, or honor. You should have won the blue ribbon at the state fair since your hog was the fattest. But there are people whom the enemy will use to steal from you in order to destroy your life through bitterness.

The second way bitterness can come into your life is through satanic attack. Think of Job. He was attacked by Satan and lost his family, his house, and his health.

When you read the first chapter of Job, you can see how terrible it is. Every time something bad happened, Job bowed down and said, "The Lord has given and the Lord has taken away. Blessed be the name of the Lord."

Some Christians use this verse to make it look like what-ever happens to you is the Lord's doing. But the Lord was not taking anything away from Job; Satan was. That's why at the end of the Book of Job, God shows up and rebukes Job. Job said a lot of things that were not accurate. So when you read this book, understand that a lot of what Job said was not inspired by God. What he said was recorded accurately, but where it came from in his heart was not of God. Job did not have the Bible like we have the Bible. He did not have all of the spiritual resources and historical data that give witness to the character of God like we have now. His knowledge of God was limited at the time of his suffering. God did reveal Himself to Job later, but at this point, Job was speaking out of hurt and bitterness.

It is a shame how bitterness sets some of us up to blame God for everything bad that has happened to us. Some believe that if God allows everything to happen, He allowed bad things to happen to them, and they ask, "God, why did You allow this to happen to me?" There are people who have left their relation-ships with God because something tragic happened and they blamed God for it. Taking it even further, there are those who stop believing that there is a God at all. They say, "If there is a God, why are all these things happening to me and my family?" What they don't understand is that God is God, but there is a devil that lives on this planet. Not everything that happens is the will of God. God allows it, but He doesn't do it.

The devil attacks families, property, and physical health. The devil has a strategy to steal, kill, and destroy every area in the life of an individual. He and his demons do so much damage to some lives because people don't know much about spiritual warfare and the demonic realm. Some aren't even saved. They don't know how to defend themselves, and they open their lives up to bitterness against others and against God. So there are a lot of bitter people on the earth who don't know how to overcome. They don't know how to stop the attacks of the enemy. The enemy just comes in and destroys.

> And a messenger came to Job and said, "The oxen were plowing, and the donkeys were feeding beside them, and the Sabeans attacked them, and took them away, and they killed the servants with the edge of the sword, and only I alone have escaped to tell you."
>
> While he was still speaking, another came and said, "The fire of God fell from heaven [this was not the fire of God; this was the enemy] and burned up the sheep and the servants and consumed them, and I alone have escaped to tell you."
>
> While he was still speaking, another came and said, "The Chaldeans formed three companies and made a raid on the camels and have taken them away. They killed the servants with the edge of the sword, and I alone have escaped to tell you."
>
> While he was still speaking, another came and said, "Your sons and your daughters were eating and drinking wine in their eldest brother's house, and suddenly a great wind came from the wilderness and struck the four corners of the house, and it fell on the young people, and they are dead; and I alone have escaped to tell you."
>
> Then Job stood up, tore his robe, and shaved his head. He fell to the ground and worshipped. He said, "Naked I came from my mother's womb, and naked will I return there. The LORD gave, and the LORD has taken away; blessed be the name of the LORD."
>
> —JOB 1:14–21

The main problem here is that the Lord didn't do this. The devil did. We have heard this taught over and over again in our churches, and for many of us, our perspective on this verse is very religious. It is time to bind the devil. When things like what happened to Job begin to come against your life, you do not kneel down and say, "The Lord is killing my family. The Lord is killing my children. The Lord burned down my house." No—you begin to access the authority you have in the Spirit through Jesus and bind the devil. Pray!

When things come against your life, you need to know how to deal with them. Otherwise you can become religious and bitter. Then you begin to point fingers at God: "God, why did You put this sickness on me?" This is what religion has taught us. Listen: God is a good God. He does not come to kill His children. It was Satan who approached God regarding Job. God simply told Satan, "Everything that Job has in your power," but then stopped and said, "but don't kill him." (See Job 1:12.) Apparently Satan didn't know that he had the power to do what he wanted to do, but he did it. Remember that Job lived before Abraham. He is one of the oldest figures in the Bible. And as I said above, Job did not have a great revelation of everything we know about God today. He didn't have the Bible—Genesis to Revelation, the Epistles, and the Prophets. He didn't have the prophetic anointing. He didn't have anything we have today. We are in a much better place today than Job was in his day. He didn't have the Holy Spirit. He wasn't saved by the blood of Jesus as we are today. Job was a man who loved and feared God, but his revelation of God was not what ours is today. So he complained.

Job got upset. I imagine him saying, "I've been serving God all these years, and now He is going to let this happen to me? I've been living clean. I know people who are worse than I am. They are driving down the road smoking cigars. They don't have any problems." Putting it in our terms today, like any number of believers, Job would have said, "They aren't speaking in tongues. They don't serve God." It's hard when you come under attack and think you are living right, and people who are living worse than you are seem to go unscathed by the devil. It doesn't seem like he touches them! But the enemy isn't fighting for those who are lost; he is fighting to destroy those who are God's. As a believer you have a target on your back, because you belong to God and Satan hates God. But God will deliver you not only from the captivity of the tragedy but also from the bitterness resulting from the tragedy, just like He did Job:

> And the LORD restored the fortunes of Job when he prayed for his friends, and also the LORD gave Job twice as much as he had before.
>
> —JOB 42:10

The truth is that life can make you bitter, but you can get deliverance and walk in the Spirit.

Bitterness affects the appetite.

Bitterness can affect your appetite.

> Another dies in the bitterness of his soul, never having eaten with pleasure.
>
> —JOB 21:25

I want to enjoy my food. I don't want gas, indigestion, and ulcers. I don't want to have to take Maalox with every meal. There are all kinds of pills, tablets, and potions on the market for people who can't eat because they're bitter—bad stomachs, bad intestines, and so forth. God doesn't want that for you. I plan to eat well all the days of my life.

Notice also that this verse suggests that some people die bitter, which leads me to the next biblical revelation on bitterness.

Bitterness opens us up to the spirit of death.

> Why is light given to the miserable, and life unto the bitter in soul, who look for death, but it is not there; and they search for it more than for hidden treasures; who rejoice exceedingly, and they are glad when they find the grave?
>
> —Job 3:20–22

You can become so bitter that you want to die. You can experience so much misery and so much bitterness in your life that you welcome death because you feel that life is not worth living. Jesus came that you might have life and that more abundantly. He did not come so you could get to a certain place in your life and say you don't want to live anymore. Life is hard, yes. There is bombing in Iraq, Afghanistan, and Englewood. Your son, your cat, and your dog may have left you. You may feel that the world is so bad or your personal circumstances are so bad that you don't want to live anymore. Listen—the joy of the Lord is your strength!

Notice in the verse that misery and bitterness are in the same category. These are demons, and you need to get them out of your life. Don't allow misery and bitterness to destroy you.

Bitterness can open us up to sexual sin.

> For the lips of an immoral woman drip as a honeycomb, and her mouth is smoother than oil. But her end is bitter as wormwood, sharp as a two-edged sword. Her feet go down to death, her steps take hold of Sheol. She does not ponder the path of life; her ways are unstable, and she does not know it.
>
> —Proverbs 5:3–6

This verse is a warning to men, instructing them to not get involved in sexual sin. Men, if you get involved with strange women, the end result is going to be bitterness in your life. This is why so many men need deliverance from bitterness. They take this bitterness into their marriages. Many men, like Esau, who feel like life has cheated them, or like Job, who have been under the attack of Satan, get involved with strange women, and when they get married, the enemy uses their bitterness to destroy their marriages. No wonder the Bible says in Colossians 3:19, "Husbands, love your wives, and do not be bitter toward them." Women, never marry a bitter man. Make sure he gets delivered first.

Foolish children can open the door to bitterness.

> A foolish son is a grief to his father, and bitterness to her who bore him.
>
> —Proverbs 17:25

This probably isn't a complete shock to anyone who has had children. Notice in this verse that bitterness comes into a mother's life if she bears a foolish son. So if your children are out doing foolish things, their actions can open the door to bitterness in your life. Satan will use anything in his power to get you bound up with bitterness. He will use your spouse, your children, other relationships, attacks, lust, or strange women. Anything in life that you can't handle opens the door for bitterness, which includes unforgiveness, hatred, anger, rage, murder, inability to eat with pleasure, and so on. We need to be delivered from bitterness.

Bitterness manifests through words.

> They sharpen their tongue like a sword, and bend their bows to shoot their arrows—bitter words, that they may shoot in secret at the blameless; suddenly they shoot at him and do not fear.
> —PSALM 64:3–4

People who are bitter speak cruel things that will hurt you. A bitter husband uses his tongue to cut up his wife. A bitter wife will do the same thing. The words of a bitter person become like arrows that pierce the hearts of others around them. That's why it is so terrible to have bitterness in a marriage. A couple who is bitter at each other will speak words to one another that are so sharp and cruel until wounds of hurt and broken-heartedness are opened up. Words hurt.

The Bible says, "Husbands, love your wives" (Eph. 5:25). Love is kind. Love speaks kind words. Then Colossians 3:19 not only directs husbands to love their wives, but also adds the warning, "Do not be bitter toward them." The Spirit of God specifically tells husbands not to be bitter toward their wives because there is a tendency and a temptation for men who are married, if they are bitter, to take it out on their wives. Bitter men are the cause of many marital problems and divorces.

This doesn't mean that women can't be bitter. Anyone can have the spirit of bitterness, but this particular scripture specifically tells men not to be bitter toward their wives. Having dealt with many women in counseling, I've talked with wives who wonder why their husbands are so abusive—verbally, physically—and treat them in a cruel way. Often the root cause of a man's mistreatment of his wife is that he has not dealt with that bitterness in his own life.

When you are bitter you become angry and abusive. Because husbands and wives are close—marriage is the closest covenant you can have—women often suffer because men have not dealt with their bitterness. A man's bitterness destroys his marriage and his family. It has an effect on his children. And while bitterness does oppress both men and women, I tend to focus more on men because in life you run across many men who have not dealt with it.

How can you tell if you are bitter? Watch your tone. Watch the way you speak. Are your words cutting and harsh, piercing, and hurtful? I have ministered to people who say, "I don't know why I talk like this." It's because there is unresolved bitterness in your heart and you take it out on others by the way you speak. Bitter words spoken by bitter people also affect how people relate to the church. Some people are hurt in the church by those who have yet to be delivered from bitterness. This is another reason why it is so important to watch what comes out of your mouth. If you have harsh and cutting words coming out of your mouth, and everyone around you is always offended and put off by what you say, you may need deliverance from the spirit of bitterness.

Entire nations can be bitter.

> For I am raising up the Chaldeans, that bitter and hasty nation which marches through the breadth of the earth, to possess dwelling places that are not theirs.
>
> —HABAKKUK 1:6

Not only can an individual be bitter, but also an entire nation. The Chaldeans or the Babylonians were a bitter nation. This caused them to be very violent and cruel. When they would go into a land and possess it, they would kill and maim. When I think of different nations—especially those in the Islamic world—and see all their hatred toward other nations, I believe bitterness is the root cause.

There are entire nations who feel they got the raw end of the deal. I believe there is no such thing as a poor nation. God has put resources in every nation—oil, diamonds, gold, and so on. Every nation has something that God has put within it to generate wealth; some governments are just corrupt, and the leaders steal all the money, leaving millions of people in poverty.

Africa, for example, is not a poor continent. There are more resources—diamonds, salt, gold, iron, cobalt, uranium, copper, bauxite, silver, petroleum, cocoa beans, woods, and tropical fruits—in Africa than on any other continent. The problem with Africa is its leaders. They have stolen millions of dollars from the people, leaving the people bitter and angry, questioning, "Why do we suffer like this?"

Sometimes the devil uses this kind of misfortune to cause people to be bitter and angry at America, wishing for its demise. Instead, they should be looking within to figure out how to solve their own problems. Bitterness will make you blame everyone else for your problems. Bitterness will always tell you, "It's their fault. You are messed up because of what they did." Bitterness will keep you from being able to see you own mistakes.

The devil destroys entire nations through bitterness.

> Why do the nations rage, and the peoples plot in vain?
> —PSALM 2:1

Don't let the devil destroy you with bitterness. We have to get delivered and walk in love. If you are bitter, don't walk in denial. Admit it and get deliverance.

Bitterness is connected to alcohol.

> They shall not drink wine with song; strong drink shall be bitter to those who drink it.
> —ISAIAH 24:9

Whenever my team and I minister to alcoholics, we always cast out demons of bitterness. They go hand-in-hand. Drugs and alcohol are other doorways that open us up to bitterness.

WE ALL NEED TO BE DELIVERED FROM BITTERNESS

God has a future for you. Bitterness, anger, and unforgiveness are destiny thieves, demons, and devils that keep you connected to your past and rob you of your future. But God wants to break you from that link of a painful past so you can move forward into the destiny He has for you.

We must pray and ask Jesus to show us any hidden or repressed memories of events in our life that are causing bitterness. There is something called memory recall or flashback that people suffer from or deal with. This is when a person remembers every bad thing that has happened to her, everything that someone has done to her. She tends to remember these things and store them up, and this often comes out when the person does the same thing to her again. That action reminds her of what has been done to her in the past.

When God forgives us, He puts our sins in the sea of forgetfulness, or the depths of the sea (Mic. 7:19). He forgets them. He doesn't remind us of them. This is what healing from God in these areas will empower us to do. This doesn't mean that you will forget the events entirely; it just means that when you recall them, you will not feel that same pain, hurt, and anger before you truly forgave and let things go. You don't want things in your past to prevent you from moving into your future.

People who have a root of bitterness also tend to be very controlling and possessive. This control and possessiveness makes them feel like they have the upper hand in a situation. They want to control things so that the results they don't want won't come into their lives. They do not want to feel the pain of rejection and disappointment, so they try to control the outcome. They think that if they are not in control, there's a higher chance they could be hurt, rejected, or experience pain. Control and domination are ways to control the outcome. What's really at play here is fear—fear of hurt, fear of failure, fear of disappointment, and so on.

The problem with trying to control the outcome of everything is that this is impossible to do. We cannot control what people do and say. What we can control is how we respond to it, the way we think, and how we allow what others do and say to affect our lives.

Be kind, gentle, and tenderhearted

There will always be knuckleheads, fools, idiots, and selfish and abusive people in life. Sinful, wicked, and ungodly people will do and say things with no regard for anyone else. There will always be people like this in the world. We meet them all the time.

You may ask yourself, "How can people be so mean? How can people do things like that?" Or, "How could someone do this to me? How could someone mistreat me like this?" You have to be careful, because this could cause you to feel that the only way you can survive living with people like that is by being mean too. A common things you may have heard is, "You have to fight fire with fire." This mind-set is not OK for a believer.

Never allow yourself to become like them, because you want the blessing of God on your life. You want to always be kind, courteous, gentle, loving, considerate, and godly. This is what God expects of you. He expects His saints to have a godly standard. The standard of most people is too low. They think they are not that bad because they compare themselves to others who are worse. Are you kind, gentle, courteous, and compassionate—not only sometimes, but on a consistent basis? This is the standard we are to grow into and live our lives by, and if it takes deliverance to be that way, then we should seek deliverance.

Unfortunately, some people are like this in their marriages. They are not kind, gentle, courteous, and compassionate to their own spouses. Sometimes married people are the meanest to each other, because they too are dealing with bitterness, hurt, and anger toward each other. I have dealt with this many times with married people. They are bitter, double-minded, and full of rejection and rebellion. They don't get delivered. Some don't know anything about deliverance because they don't go to a church that does deliverance. So they carry all these things into their marriages, and before you know it they are fighting like cats and dogs. This is not the character of God demonstrated.

Not just for women

Being kind, gentle, and tender is not just something that women should do. Men need to be this way as well toward their wives, their children, and others they relate to. The worst combination is when a person is mean and stubborn, which means he or she is going to hold on to that mean disposition and will not change. If someone tells you that you are mean and unkind, you ought to at least consider it and say you'll work on it. Get some prayer. Get some help. Realize it is not godly.

God is kind to you.

The Bible says, "Let all bitterness, wrath, anger, outbursts, and blasphemies, with all malice, be taken away from you. And be kind one to another, tenderhearted, forgiving one another, just as God in Christ also forgave you" (Eph. 4:31–32). Notice the contrast between the two verses. In the first verse you see bitterness, wrath, anger, arguing, and malice. In the second verse you see kind, tenderhearted, and forgiving, as God has forgiven you.

Aren't you glad God wasn't bitter against you? What if you came to God and He said, "I know you are not in My face." "I know this is not who I think it is." "Angels, you'd better hold Me back." But this is not what happens. God is kind to us. He doesn't abuse or mistreat us.

LIFE IS WORTH LIVING

One of the ways you know you have been delivered from unforgiveness, anger, bitterness, and resentment is if you are kind. You know how to speak to people and be courteous and respectful, in public and in private. You're not raging. How you deal with the things that happen to you can determine the quality of your life. You don't want to be like King Solomon, the man who had everything. He concluded at the end of his life that life was terrible and not worth living. Read Ecclesiastes; it is one of the most depressing books. In essence Solomon ended his life saying, "I had everything. But everything is vanity. Everything vexes me. Life is the vexation of spirit." He said, "Therefore I hated life" (Eccles. 2:17, kjv). What a statement! He also said that "with all the things people go through, it's better to be dead. Even better than that is never having been born." (See Ecclesiastes 4:2–3.) Could it be that he got bitter and angry because of his disobedience and rebellion?

That is not an abundant life. God wants you to enjoy life, joy, peace, righteousness, favor, relationships, your children, your spouse, your family, wealth, prosperity, food, eating, drinking, and fellowship. I am not saying that enjoying life is all about having fun, but you can even enjoy working.

It's important that we allow the Lord to heal us, because life can throw some bad stuff at us. The joy of the Lord is our strength. He will give us the garment of praise for the spirit of heaviness. We don't have to stay bitter, mean, angry, and unforgiving. With God, we can sleep at night. When we are healed and whole, and not going around mistreating people, we shouldn't have to worry about people hunting us down.

In your restored state, if you have offended someone, you know how to go to him and ask him to forgive you. And if he comes to you, you know how to humbly say, "I'm sorry. Forgive me." If you have been wronged, you know how to go to the person or forgive him. You don't have to become bitter.

If there is something you can't seem to let go, go to someone who is strong and mature in the Lord and get some prayer and deliverance. When you can't let something go, that is a devil gaining a foothold in your life, and it needs to come out in the name of Jesus. You don't want bitterness to destroy your life.

REJECT BITTERNESS

Bitterness is like a poison to your system. It is called wormwood or gall. Wormwood is very bitter. When you taste something bitter, your taste buds will reject it. Your body discerns it. Your tongue discerns it. And your body rejects it.

You should really be the same way—before bitterness gets into your system, you should reject it. It should not be comfortable to your spiritual taste. Of course there are things like bitter candies out there. People like them. You can get used to bitter things. Your taste buds say no, but it can become an acquired taste, like vinegar. No one wants to drink a glass of vinegar. Your taste buds and your system reject that.

You should reject bitterness in the same way. You should not allow bitterness to contaminate your spirit. Declare, "I will not be angry, upset, and revengeful. I will not be full of hatred. I will not be miserable. I will not become old and grumpy. I want to enjoy life. I want to enjoy food, friends, and fellowship. I want to enjoy church. I want to enjoy my family."

CHAPTER 7

FORGIVE AND BE HEALED

The Connection Between Double-Mindedness and Infirmity

He was despised and rejected of men, a man of sorrows and acquainted with grief. And we hid, as it were, our faces from him; he was despised, and we did not esteem him. Surely he has borne our grief and carried our sorrows; Yet we esteemed him stricken, smitten of God, and afflicted. But he was wounded for our transgressions, he was bruised for our iniquities; the chastisement of our peace was upon him, and by his stripes we are healed.

—ISAIAH 53:3–5

I N THIS CHAPTER we are going to look at some of the common reasons people get sick beyond just the physical reasons. This spiritual perspective does not discount the simple idea that sometimes we do get sick, and it is not always demonic. There are cut-and-dry physical reasons why viruses, germs, and bacteria affect our bodies. Still, there are instances when we cannot ignore that a sickness or disease is spiritually rooted, and we need deliverance in order to be healed.

When a person suffers from colds and flu on a consistent basis, even though these may be viruses or bacterial infections that can be medically diagnosed, often it is the result of a weakened immune system. The immune system has been compromised, and it limits the person's ability to fight off germs, viruses, or bacteria. Although these illnesses are common to everyone, your body is designed to fight off these things. But there are some people whose immune systems are weakened because of self-rejection or some other spiritual problem. They stay ill.

I am working to make this distinction because I do know that when I teach this from a deliverance perspective, people may say that I am blaming everything on a demon and ignoring science or medicine. I do not believe that science or medicine is an enemy. I believe that doctors can do quite a bit for people. But I also know that much of what is called medicine today is simply prescribing drugs that don't heal. They only cover up or take away the symptoms. They do not get to the root problem. Sometimes the root problem, which could be spiritual, is not what the doctors are trained to diagnose. Real medicine heals people. For example, if you get an infection of some kind, and you take penicillin and it heals you, that's good. There's nothing wrong with that. That's legitimate. But then there is the spiritual side.

GETTING TO THE ROOT

In the opening verse above, take note that when it says, "he has borne our grief and carried our sorrows," the literal translation of *grief* and *sorrows* means "sickness" and "disease." I believe this is the correct translation, because in Matthew 8:16–17, Matthew quotes Isaiah 53, saying, "When the even was come, they brought unto him many that were possessed with devils: and he cast out the spirits with his word, and healed all that were sick: That it might be fulfilled which was spoken by Esaias the prophet, saying, Himself took our infirmities, and bare our sicknesses" (KJV).

Jesus fulfilled Isaiah's prophecy of His bearing our griefs and carrying our sorrows by casting out demons and healing the sick. The translation of Isaiah 53 is not completely off, as sickness and infirmity do cause grief and sorrow.

Notice also the connection in Isaiah 53:3 between Jesus's rejection and His carrying of our griefs and sorrows (sicknesses and infirmities). Rejection is often the root cause of much sorrow and grief, and it is also the root cause of much sickness and infirmity. When you suffer from rejection, you also may have to deal with self-rejection and self-hatred. This happens a lot of the time because of how people deal with what others think or feel about them. But you should never judge yourself based on what others feel about you. You should only judge yourself based on what God feels about you. However, most people are not equipped from a young age to deal with rejection. It is very hurtful and painful, especially for a child who feels rejected by a mother or father. Sometimes even when they are not actually rejected, they feel as though they are rejected. There are all kinds of rejection, including racial, societal, and gender rejection. Rejection is one of the worst things the enemy can cause to happen in a person's life. It opens us up to so much.

I teach on rejection a lot, and one of the best resources I can recommend for people to learn about rejection is *Excuse Me, Your Rejection Is Showing* by deliverance pioneers Phil and Noel Gibson. They call rejection the masterpiece of Satan. Rejection is one of the ways Satan tries to destroy everyone who comes into the world. Rejection is a doorkeeper. It is a root problem, a root demon. As I have already stated, when it comes to deliverance you have to get to the root. The axe is laid to the root (Matt. 3:10; Luke 3:9). You can break branches off. You can break symptoms off. But unless you go to the root of rejection and pull it up from there, it will grow right back like a weed.

Deliverance ministry is designed to get to root problems. The problem with roots is that you can't see them with the natural eye. They are often hidden underground, but you know they are there. Often the problems that people have are hidden from the natural eye and can only be discerned by the Spirit of God, by someone with discernment who is able to see what cannot ordinarily be seen.

Medical doctors primarily deal with empirical evidence. They deal with what they can see on charts and tests. They don't always deal with rejection, anger, and bitterness. Many medical professionals are just now beginning to accept that there is a strong relationship between the health or our spirits and the health of our bodies and minds. The Bible says in 3 John 1:2, "Beloved, I pray that all may go well with you and that you may be in good health, even as your soul is well."

Psychiatrists may get into some of the psychological reasons why a person is suffering with something, but usually traditional medicine doesn't. Unfortunately, unless you have an understanding of deliverance and the spirit realm, chances are you won't be able to diagnose what you or the people around you are dealing with. You may feel that you just have to get over whatever it is by faith. Then if you remain ill, you may feel guilt and shame, falling into the belief that your lack of faith is what's keeping you sick. Now you can get delivered and healed by faith. I'm not against that. Still you must gain a full understanding of God's deliverance and deal with the root problem: demons.

The Bible doesn't give us every sickness and disease by name. It doesn't use our modern terminology to specify each illness or disease. It does tell us that one of the ways Jesus took or lifted the people's sicknesses and infirmities was by casting out demons with His word and healing all those who were sick (Matt. 8:16). Often what we do here is focus on Matthew 8:17, which says, "He Himself took our infirmities and bore our sicknesses," and with a word of faith type understanding we try to confess it by faith. This is fine, but often we don't look at that verse within the context of verse 16: "...they brought to Him many who were possessed with demons. And He cast out the spirits with His word, and healed all who were sick." We tend to disconnect these two verses. But the proper application here is that healing from sickness and infirmity often comes through casting out demons.

Some of us have accepted the belief that as Christians, we can't have demons. But we can. A person is made up of three parts—spirit, soul, and body. Understanding the three parts that make up a human will help you to understand how it is that a Christian can be filled with the Holy Spirit and still have a demon. The Holy Spirit dwells in the spirit part of man. Demons take up residence in the soul. This is why our minds have to be renewed. Demons take up certain areas of your life. They don't possess you—spirit, soul, and body. Some people may say, "Well, God and the devil can't be in the same place." I can quickly debunk that myth. God is omnipresent on the earth. He is everywhere, yet demons are here. So if God and the devil can't be in the same place, how do we have demons on the earth? We try to explain the spirit realm like the natural realm, but entirely different rules apply in the spirit realm.

This is why I think it is important to join these two concepts—faith and deliverance—and operate powerfully in both to experience true freedom.

Sickness and Infirmity Are Tormentors

> Then his master, after he had summoned him, said to him, "O you wicked servant! I forgave you all that debt because you pleaded with me. Should you not also have had compassion on your fellow servant, even as I had pity on you?" His master was angry and delivered him to the jailers until he should pay all his debt.
>
> So also My heavenly Father will do to each of you, if from your heart you do not forgive your brother for his trespasses.
>
> —MATTHEW 18:32–25

If you recall in Matthew 18:23–35, the man who did not forgive his brother was handed over to tormentors. Tormentors represent demons. In Old Covenant times, when a person was in debt he could be jailed. Today we don't have debtor's prison.

We can be sued or our wages garnished, but we won't be put in jail. But in the Bible days, if you had bad debt you were put in jail and tormented. Herein is a spiritual principle. We definitely don't want to live our lives being tormented by the enemy. So we often need to be healed from the root of bitterness. The memories of bad things that have happened need to be healed by forgiveness. This forgiveness is the gift of God.

Because many people will not forgive, they suffer from a lot of physical conditions from which they are not being healed. Sickness and disease are tormenting.

BITTERNESS AND UNFORGIVENESS ARE KILLING YOU

The root cause for many diseases is unforgiveness and bitterness. Medical doctors, scientists, and researchers are finding conclusive evidence that there is a much closer connection between the mind, body, and spirit than was once thought. These are not necessarily new findings when you study the Word and receive revelation from God about root spirits that take hold of us. The connection between rejection/rebellion/bitterness and physical and psychological illness is not new in deliverance ministry. But the good thing is that for those who need it, there is a growing library of research proving the connection between double-mindedness and physical diseases and illnesses.

In our own ministry we have found that bitterness, resentment, and unforgiveness open the door for arthritis, cancer, autoimmune disorders, and many other ailments. But in my almost forty years in deliverance ministry, two of the main health problems I've found in people who are bitter are cancer and arthritis. I do not mean to imply that everyone who has these diseases is dealing with bitterness or rejection or another double-mindedness demon. What I am saying is that these spiritual issues *could be* a root cause, and with the leading of the Spirit we have seen people healed from these diseases during deliverance ministry.

Many of these ailments begin to show up in people as they start getting older. Over the course of their lives, they don't forgive, they hold on to grudges, they don't release people, they hold on to anger, and they don't get deliverance. Then after so many years their bodies begin to be affected by bitterness, resentment, and anger. There is a profound effect on your body when bitterness is in your system.

Anger and rage, both rooted in bitterness, have pronounced effects on the autonomic nervous system and the immune system. Your immune system, of course, is the part of you that protects you from disease and sickness. When your immune system is compromised, your body does not have the ability to fight off infections, sicknesses, and diseases. When you are full of anger, rage, or fear, the adrenaline level in your blood is increased, which gets your body ready to fight or run. This is known as the fight or flight syndrome. The increase of adrenaline causes contraction and spasm in the smooth muscles (the autonomic muscles) of the intestines, stomach, bladder, and blood vessels, which subsequently causes many physical symptoms if this reaction remains engaged over long periods of time. For many people in society, being wound up with anger, fear, and even stress is a normal everyday occurrence, yet this is a destructive place to be.

Bitterness has pronounced effects on the immune system by lowering your resistance to disease and altering your immune system so that allergies occur. Autoimmune responses occur when you become allergic to certain parts of your own body. This is when your body turns on itself and attacks itself such as with arthritis, fibromyalgia, lupus, certain heart issues, some cancers, type 1 diabetes, and various allergies. These are what were previously called "collagen diseases," now called autoimmune diseases.

Since the root of bitterness stems from repressed anger and rage, and there is usually a root of unforgiveness, which can be pointed toward yourself, others, or God, every area of your body is a potential target for the enemy. The following is a list of physical conditions that result from bitterness and unforgiveness as well as other demons found in the rejection, rebellion, and bitterness clusters.[1] While there may be some overlap because we are so interconnected, I categorized the various infirmities by body system. The list is not exhaustive, and I am not attempting to give medical advice or diagnoses. This information is for you to take to the Lord and seek the guidance of the Holy Spirit concerning how your body can be affected by spirits that operate within double-mindedness.

CARDIOVASCULAR SYSTEM—HEART DISEASE OR DISORDERS

Issues commonly associated with heart problems include heart attack, infirmity, death, heart blockage, broken rhythm in the heart, rapid heartbeat, panicky feeling in the heart, fibrillation, pain in the chest, breastbone pain, cardiac arrest, and the like. Heart problems are commonly rooted in fear and doubt.

Issues such as aneurysms and strokes, which are cause by ruptured blood vessels, are commonly rooted in rage, anger, hostility, self-rejection, and bitterness. Other heart issues brought on by fear, stress, anxiety, paranoia, and anger include angina (lack of blood flow to the heart tissue) and high blood pressure.

Cholesterol problems are commonly rooted in anger, paranoia, and fear; withholding, inadequacy, insignificance, sorrow, anger, self-deprecation (constantly putting oneself down).

Congestive heart failure is also commonly rooted in fear and anxiety as well as bitterness and self-rejection. The Bible says, "Men's hearts [fail] them for fear" (Luke 21:26, KJV).

DIGESTIVE SYSTEM—STOMACH, INTESTINAL, OR EATING DISORDERS

I've found that if you can't enjoy food, you really can't enjoy life. So we definitely want this system of the body healed. Sometimes we get so deep spiritually that we overlook the natural things in life. Ecclesiastes 3:13 says, "And also that everyone should eat and drink and experience good in all their labor. This is a gift of God." Eating, drinking, and enjoying life are gifts from God, so you definitely don't want your gut messed up. Of course, some digestive issues, like those caused by food poisoning or foodborne bacteria, can be simply a result of eating bad food. They may not always be a result of demons. But there are other digestive issues that are directly related to demonic oppression.

If your intestinal system is messed up, it takes away one of the most enjoyable pleasures of life, which is eating and drinking and enjoying this with other people. This is not about sitting at home alone eating ten Big Macs with the door locked. You don't want to do that. In the Bible eating and drinking represents fellowship with friends and family. Here are some digestive and eating disorders that need to be dealt with in deliverance.

Anorexia, bulimia, gluttony, and weight issues

Addiction to food can be a spiritual problem. Food replaces love. Food addiction and eating disorders can become forms of overabundant self-love. They are rooted in self-hatred, self-rejection, self-bitterness, lack of self-esteem, insecurity, addiction, compulsive behavior, self-pity, idleness, self-reward, fear of disapproval, rejection, perceived lack of love, frustration, nervousness, resentment, and pride. This set of disorders manifests in various ways, such as binge eating, secret abnormal eating, compulsive eating, non-spiritual fasting, and purging what food had been eaten.

The person dealing with this becomes "driven" in everything and feels that he or she has to perform to be accepted. Some believe that eating disorders could also be genetic, but the root of what was passed down from that ancestor is still spiritual. Eating disorders can also be the result of a spirit of control, matriarchal witchcraft, etc., and are put in the same category as self-mutilation, which is a result of bitterness.

An eating disorder is a hidden addiction to food, and those who suffer from it

- desire to eat but won't because they fear they won't be able to stop;

- feel of no value; and

- feel rejected, unloved (also toward self).

Intestinal diseases and digestion

These issues include diverticulitis, Crohn's disease, ulcerative colitis, acid reflux, mucous colitis, spastic colon, and the like. These issues are commonly rooted in fear, abandonment, and rejection, which results in self-rejection, self-bitterness, and self-hatred—not accepting oneself due to a broken relationship. The spiritual force causes the body to dry up the liquids that should soften the excretion, so it hardens instead.[2] When our relationships with family members are broken, we blame ourselves, and guilt and condemnation come in. At other times we don't blame ourselves, but we allow other people to blame us. Then we get hit with guilt, shame, and rejection. These things have a physical effect on our bodies.

One of the more serious intestinal diseases is Crohn's disease, which is commonly rooted in self-hate and self-rejection. Crohn's disease is an autoimmune disease that causes the white blood cells to eat the lining of the colon, causing ulceration and massive loss of flesh. White blood cells, called "killer T cells," are a significant part of your immune system. They normally function as part of the immune system, helping you stay healthy. So when they turn against the healthy cells in your body, this is a sign of self-rejection and self-hate.

Notice how much I am talking about self-hate, self-rejection, and guilt—guilt because of not performing perfectly to gain love, affection, and acceptance from an unloving parent. Colon cancer is another intestinal tract issue that is commonly rooted in bitterness and slander with the tongue. The power of death and life is in the tongue.

Finally, ulcers (connected to fear, stress, and anxiety) open the door for parasites, bacteria, and other organisms to attack various areas of the body.

IMMUNE AND LYMPHATIC SYSTEMS—COLDS, FLU, BACTERIAL AND VIRAL ILLNESSES, SOME CANCERS, SOME AUTOIMMUNE DISORDERS

You need a healthy body to have a healthy immune system, but a healthy body is the result of a healthy soul. A healthy soul is a delivered soul.

Autoimmune disease[3]

> An autoimmune disorder occurs when the body's immune system attacks and destroys healthy body tissue by mistake. There are more than 80 types of autoimmune disorders... When you have an autoimmune disorder, your immune system does not distinguish between healthy tissue and antigens. As a result, the body sets off a reaction that destroys normal tissues.[4]

Autoimmune disorders include type 1 diabetes, multiple sclerosis, rheumatoid arthritis, lupus, fibromyalgia, Crohn's disease, thyroid disorders, and other white blood cell deviant behaviors.[5] You can find a full list of autoimmune diseases here: http://www.aarda.org/autoimmune-information/list-of-diseases/.

> ([Autoimmune disorders are] the manifestations of
> self-hatred, self-guilt, self-conflict, self-rejection, self-
> bitterness, self-conflict, etc.) As the person attacks him-
> self spiritually, the body attacks the body physically, and
> the enemy joins in. When we attack ourselves with self-
> hate and bitterness, we are giving the white corpuscles
> permission to attack us as well, and giving the enemy
> permission to do the same![6]

Hatred is what causes someone to attack you. Self-hatred is
what causes you to turn on yourself and attack yourself; this
is what autoimmune disease is. Many times the root of an
autoimmune disease is demonic. The demons of self-hate, self-
rejection, bitterness, guilt, and shame are physically attacking
your body. These demons cause us not to love ourselves. You
would be surprised at the number of people who do not love
themselves. The Bible says that we are to love our neighbor as
we love ourselves. How can you love your neighbor if you don't
love yourself? You can't. Some people have suffered so much
rejection that they don't love themselves. Their image of themselves is based on what someone else said to or about them, or
did to them—and it was not loving.

Diabetes

Diabetes is commonly rooted in a critical and discontented
spirit—one that is unsatisfied, angry, rejected, self-hating,
abused, rejected, abandoned—and feelings of guilt. Again, let
me state that I am not saying that if you have diabetes you
have all of this. I am not being dogmatic. I am saying that it is
commonly rooted in these issues. There can be strictly physical
aspects to this.

Rejection roots itself through this disease due to rejection, usually from a father or husband or a man in general. Fathers generally set the emotional welfare of a child. Being rejected by one's father is the most devastating thing that can happen in a person's life. Fathers are ordained by God to set the stability of a child. Many of us come from homes where the father was absent, abusive, or unloving, or abdicated his responsibilities. So the enemy uses the absence of a man or father to affect children, causing rejection.

Rejection can also happen from a mother. But men carry more authority in the home than women do. The husband is set as the head of the wife (Eph. 5:23). There is an attack on men and on families, and children are coming from unstable homes, resulting in a fear of man and a hatred of men.

This rejection sometimes manifests in the body as type 1 diabetes, which is when white blood vessels seek and destroy the pancreas, causing an insulin deficiency. This is an autoimmune disease affecting the central nervous system.[7] Fatigue, lethargy, overeating, depression, and insomnia that accompany it are characteristically caused by fear, anxiety, and stress. Also, diabetes can be a manifestation of a type A or performance- or perfection-driven personality.

The US National Library of Medicine further supports this:

> Conditions such as depression, and eating, cognitive and behavioural disorders may pre-date the onset of diabetes or present during the course of illness. There are additional challenges when diabetes develops in children and young people with pre-existing emotional and psychological difficulties, such as severe conduct or attachment difficulties, autism spectrum disorder or family dysfunction.[8]

Remember, we highlighted perfectionism as being part of the rejection personality. These people feel that if they can perform well enough or perfectly enough, then they will be accepted. But this is what causes diabetes to be progressive. In this case you would need to cast out the spirits of inheritance and the spirit of diabetes, pray for the healing of the pancreas, command healing and restoration to all body parts that were damaged, command the chemical and electrical frequencies to be in harmony and in balance, and command the body to absorb any sick cells. Pray for the wisdom to be healed and delivered.

Colds, flu, and viruses

These illnesses are commonly rooted in stress, brokenheartedness, self-doubt, guilt, and other issues contributing to a broken immune system, which opens us up to any floating virus. The virus itself may not be a spiritually rooted problem, but how it gets in can be. Protect yourself by repenting, especially during stressful times, forgiving others, and forgiving yourself. Monitor your thoughts and the intentions of your heart daily. Every little thing matters. Keep things resolved and the virus will not take root. Casting demons out is essential.

Leukemia

There are different kinds of leukemia. Each one can have a different root. Spiritual roots may be "deep-rooted bitterness, resentment and self-hatred coming from rejection by a father."[9] Many of these sicknesses and diseases are related to fathers and mothers. The Bible says, "Honor your father and your mother, that your days may be long" (Exod. 20:12). It is very important to honor your parents. "But what if they are wrong?" you may ask. They might be. But you cannot allow yourself to get bitter and angry, as this will destroy you. You have to honor them even if they are wrong. They are still your parents. You love them and honor them. Don't allow the enemy to cut your life short.

INTEGUMENTARY SYSTEM—SKIN DISORDERS

Skin problems such as acne, rashes, boils, eczema, shingles, and psoriasis are commonly rooted in fear and anxiety, self-hatred, lack of self-esteem, and conflict with identity. These skin disorders are basically overactive histamine responses.

MUSCULAR SYSTEM

Muscle tension, spasms, and pain are commonly rooted in fear, anxiety, and stress.

NERVOUS SYSTEM—BRAIN, NERVE, OR SENSORY DISORDERS

Ear issues such as ringing in the ears, though often a result of an accident or overexposure to loud noise, can also be rooted in witchcraft and the occult. Cast these spirits out and repent to receive healing.

Eye problems are commonly associated with grief. Psalm 6:7 and 31:9 talk about the eye being consumed with grief because of one's enemies. This grief may be specifically related to broken relationships.

Tension and migraine headaches are commonly rooted in internalized conflict. For example, a person may be mad at themselves for not handling situations or people the way God wanted them to.

Multiple sclerosis is commonly rooted in deep self-hatred, shame, self-bitterness, and self-rejection.

REPRODUCTIVE SYSTEM—BREAST, OVARIAN, AND PROSTATE CANCERS; INFERTILITY; LACK OF SEXUAL FUNCTION; AND OTHER MALE OR FEMALE REPRODUCTIVE ISSUES

- Breast cancer—commonly a result of "deep-rooted bitterness and resentment either with a mother or one or more sisters."[10]

- Ovarian cancer—stems from resentment with the mother. Caused by promiscuity or hatred at being female. Not accepting yourself as a woman. Resulting from a "woman's hatred for herself and her sexuality; unclean and unloving demons accusing her in the cleanness of her sexuality can lead to self-bitterness and self-loathing concerning sexuality."[11]

- Prostate or uterine cancer—rooted in anger, guilt, self-hatred, self-bitterness; the need to be loved; being rejected; promiscuity; uncleanness; self-conflict with being a man; self-rejection; and self-hatred.[12]

The issues men and women suffer in this area bring to mind lesbianism and homosexuality: these are self-rejection issues;

you are not accepting the way God made you. Gender iden-
tification issues also come to mind: If you are a woman and
you want to be a man, or if you are a man who wants to be
a woman, that is self-rejection. You must accept the way God
made you. If you are a woman, God had a purpose in creating
you that way. The same applies for if you were born male.

RESPIRATORY SYSTEM—ASTHMA, ALLERGIES, AND OTHER BREATHING ISSUES

Allergies affect most body systems. Of course, with allergies
there is a component that is strictly physical and not spiritually
connected, such as mold, mildew, and a higher pollen count
during certain times of the year. But remember that allergies
are basically part of your immune system. That's why at certain times of the year some people's immune systems just go
crazy—too much ragweed or mold or something in the air.

In the spirit realm allergies are rooted in spirits of fear, lack
of forgiveness, feelings of inadequacy, insignificance, sorrow,
anxiety, and stress. Stress can cause your immune system to
be compromised. "A merry heart does good like a medicine,
but a broken spirit dries the bones" (Prov. 17:22). Allergies are
connected with the bone marrow being dried up!

SKELETAL SYSTEM—BONE DISEASES AND DISORDERS

The Bible addresses bone problems. In Psalm 31:10 it says that
iniquity causes our bodies to be weakened and our bones to
waste away. The Bible says that if we walk according to the

Word, it will be health to our navel and marrow to our bones. (See Proverbs 3:8, ASV.) I have listed a couple of bone issues to help you see the spiritual roots of some of the bone disorders you or someone you know may be dealing with:

- Osteoporosis—commonly rooted in bitterness, envy, and jealousy. (See Proverbs 12:4; 14:30.) There can also be a controlling nature within the person that comes from an evil root of matriarchal leadership in the home.[13]

- Rheumatoid arthritis—an autoimmune disease rooted in bitterness and unforgiveness toward another, dead or alive, resulting in self-rejection, self-hate coupled with guilt. White blood cells attack the connective cartilage of the joints and eat it.[14] Stress, guilt, bitterness, not forgiving oneself, fear of self, lack of forgiving others, and not wanting to face self-conflict all contribute to rheumatoid arthritis.

HEALING THE BITTER WATERS

When they came to Marah, they could not drink of the waters of Marah, for they were bitter. Therefore, the name of it was called Marah. So the people murmured against Moses, saying, "What shall we drink?"

And he cried to the LORD, and the LORD showed him a tree. When he had thrown it into the waters, the waters were made sweet.

There He made for them a statute and an ordinance, and there He tested them. He said, "If you diligently listen to the voice of the LORD your God, and do what is right in His sight, and give ear to His commandments, and keep all His statutes, I will not afflict you with any of the diseases with which I have afflicted the Egyptians. For I am the LORD who heals you."

—EXODUS 15:23–26

It is here, at the bitter waters of Marah, that God first reveals Himself as Jehovah Rapha, the Lord our Healer. Here is where the Lord also gives us the connection between healing and bitterness. The name *Marah*, used in the verse above, is directly translated as "bitter" and refers to the bitter spring or pool of water that the people of Israel encountered after their exodus from Egypt.[15] The word *marah*, used throughout the Old Testament, means bitter, change, be disobedient, disobey, grievously, provocation, provoking. Going further it is used in a causative connotation: to make bitter, to cause to rebel, to provoke. Then figuratively it means to resist, to rebel.[16]

In order to heal the waters of Marah, God instructed Moses to throw a tree into the waters, and the waters were made sweet (Exod. 15:23–25). The tree represents Jesus Christ and His cross. Two of the redemptive things Jesus suffered on the cross was being bruised and rejected. Part of His suffering for us was being rejected by men, rejected by His own Israel. He was despised and not esteemed. So part of the redemption that Christ came to bring, part of His suffering, was rejection from His own people.

So it seems that within redemption, healing, restoration, salvation, and sufferings of Christ, the element that deals with rejection is always present. That means whatever we are dealing with in life, whether rejection, hurt, or bitterness, we can get healed and restored and be made whole. The redemption of the Cross sweetens the waters. The tree in the form of a cross upon which Christ was hung sweetens the life of every person who accepts His sacrifice. Through salvation, which includes deliverance from bitterness, anger, resentment, rejection, pride, and rebellion, life becomes sweet.

That's what deliverance is all about. Deliverance is salvation. Deliverance is healing. Deliverance is restoration. God wants you whole, not living your life messed up. Jesus saves, heals, delivers, restores, and makes whole.

God is a physician. He puts you back together again so that you can have life and have it more abundantly. He doesn't want to you have to carry all these hurts throughout life. You definitely do not want to grow old being bitter. You don't want to grow old being sick and mean. People wonder why it seems that some older people are so mean. It's just a manifestation of bitterness. They live all the years of their lives without releasing any of the hardship they've been through, so by the time they reach a certain age they are mean and grouchy. We sometimes think that this is just a part of getting old. No, it is not. Those are just old demons.

You do not have to be old and bitter and mean and sick and all messed up. If you get old and feel you have a right to hate everybody, then the devil has a right to destroy your life: "I have a right to mess you up." This is not the way God wants His people to live.

So then, it is no wonder that God, in His great love for us all, revealed Himself to the people of Israel as their healer at the bitter waters of Marah. Bitterness and healing go hand-in-hand. Israel had just come out of Egypt, out of four hundred years of bondage. When you've been in bondage that long, there's a great chance that you will harbor unforgiveness and bitterness toward the people that put you in bondage.

You Can Forgive

As I pointed out in the previous chapter, bitterness is repressed anger or rage that is produced by rebellion and stubbornness. Many times stubbornness is manifested as a refusal to forgive someone. The Bible says, "Stubbornness is as iniquity and idolatry" (1 Sam. 15:23). This is a message to us. When we stubbornly refuse to let someone go—when we refuse to release and forgive them, saying instead, "I'll never forgive that person. I will always hate them. I'll not release it. I'll not let it go. You don't know what happened to me. You don't know what they did to me. I have a right to hold on to this. I have a right to be angry. I have a right to be upset with this individual. I will not forgive them"—this means you are stubbornly holding on to unforgiveness, even though God commands us to forgive and release people.

Some people think that they can't forgive because they don't feel like it. The truth of it is, there are a lot of things you have to do by faith. You can't go by how you feel, because you may feel like punching the person's lights out. For you, forgiveness will not only be an act of faith; it will also need to be an act of your will. You may find yourself having to act and say that you forgive them, and then—with God's strength—actually do it. Forgiving and setting people free will bring healing to your body, mind, and spirit.

PROSPER AND BE IN HEALTH

Going through this list of diseases, you may have found that guilt showed up a lot. Many diseases are rooted in guilt. Guilt is one of the worst things you can allow to control your life. Guilt comes from condemnation, shame, unworthiness, embarrassment, low self-esteem, and feelings of inferiority (low class, bottom of the barrel, always last place, insecure, never good enough). Guilt is the root of countless diseases and unhappiness. There are people who live their lives feeling guilty about things they did years ago. They have never forgiven themselves for something they did or did not do. They literally punish themselves. They feel unworthy, ashamed, and embarrassed, which often turns into self-rejection.

Guilt is a terrible demon, and you have to be delivered from it. You can ask God to forgive you, and you can ask the people you may have hurt to forgive you, but the most important thing you need to do is forgive yourself. This is the hardest part for many people. They believe God forgives them and other people forgive them, but they can't forgive themselves.

We have all done things that we are not proud of, but we must remember that when we've done all we can do to make things right, Jesus is our righteousness. He covers us. If we don't get this into our spirits, then we are open to being afflicted by many sicknesses and diseases, because there is a connection between the spirit, soul, and body. The Bible says, "I pray that in all respects you may prosper and be in good health, just as your soul prospers" (3 John 1:2, NAS). Your soul is your mind, will, and emotions. If your soul is not healthy and you are overcome with hurt, shame, guilt, fear, and rejection, your body will eventually be affected. It doesn't always happen overnight. The longer you carry these things, the more damage they do.

This is why many of these diseases manifest in older age. Sometimes younger bodies can resist some of the spiritual ails better than older bodies that have carried the issues longer. I personally don't believe that as you get older you have to become sickly. I don't believe God designed our bodies to break down and us to suffer. But I believe that this is why many people become sick in their older age; they shoulder guilt, resentment, anger, and other negative spirits for years and years until their bodies begin to manifest these spirits physically.

Self-rejection, self-pity, self-bitterness, and self-hatred also showed up often in the list above. Some people don't think these spirits are that bad when compared with a demon like lust. But the thing is, they can do just as much damage to your life as lust can. They may not be moral sins like lust, fornication, adultery, or homosexuality. We tend to see moral demons as the worst kind. But with demons like self-rejection and self-pity, we just pat the person on the back who is dealing with those issues and tell them, "Just hang in there. Everything will be all right." We pet those demons, but they are the kind that cause people to destroy themselves. We need to take them seriously and be set free.

I didn't cover every sickness and disease in this chapter, but I did uncover the root issues of the bigger health issues more common to us all. From there we can see trends and begin to pinpoint what kind of deliverance we need to receive to obtain complete healing.

In many of these issues like cancer, arthritis, type 1 diabetes, and certain heart conditions, we find that the body is attacking itself, and we have uncovered spiritual reasons why it would do this. Obviously I don't know all the ramifications of sickness and disease. I am not claiming any medical expertise. But what I am doing is pointing out the very real connection between our spiritual condition and our health.

There is still a lot that even the doctors are learning concerning this connection. There are many illnesses, like autoimmune diseases, for which it is hard to find the physical cause. People go their whole lives, sometimes, with no diagnosis. What doctors and scientific researchers are discovering is the link between the spirit, mind, and body in many of these cases. The common issues that you can see from what I have listed here—repressed anger, unforgiveness, resentment, bitterness, guilt, shame, fear, insecurity, trauma, abuse, identity issues, and so on—are being listed as causal factors in many diseases doctors had in the past found difficult to diagnose and treat.

This is why we must go to the Lord for His wisdom on how to overcome these problems. His gifts—word of knowledge, word of wisdom, and discerning of spirits—and His Spirit can give us insight into how to heal many of these issues even beyond what the doctors are able to do. You must depend on the Spirit of God to find healing and deliverance from every enemy.

CHAPTER 8

DIVIDE AND CONQUER

Deliverance From Double-Mindedness

The LORD *your God will drive out those nations before you, little by little. You will not be able to destroy them all at once... But the* LORD *your God will deliver them to you and will throw them into a great confusion until they are destroyed.*

—DEUTERONOMY 7:22–23

T HE STRATEGY TO attack double-mindedness is to separate rejection from rebellion. Attack the rejection stronghold, and attack the root of bitterness, which is the core of the rebellion stronghold. Then attack the rebellion stronghold. It is helpful to be familiar with the patterns and clusters of demons that work within the false personalities. Remember, this deliverance takes time, little by little (Exod. 23:29–30). The spirits under rejection and rebellion strengthen them, and they are weakened as the others are driven out.

Those who are delivered from double-mindedness are sometimes left with no personality. They must have time to develop one with the help of Christ or they will have nothing to fall back on. They should develop the following:

- Ability to esteem others without impure motives
- Accountability
- Authenticity
- Balance
- Completeness in the things of God
- Concentration
- Confidence
- Courage
- Deep appreciation for spiritual blessings
- Devotion
- Faith
- Flexibility to the Holy Spirit
- Gentleness
- Heart for God and His people
- Honesty
- Honor
- Integrity
- Joy
- Kindness
- Love
- Loyalty
- Meekness
- Obedience
- Patience
- Positive self-esteem
- Punctuality
- Resourcefulness
- Responsibility
- Reverence
- Security
- Self-assurance
- Self-discipline
- Self-respect
- Single-mindedness
- Submission to God and leadership
- Thoroughness
- Trustworthiness
- Truthfulness
- Virtue
- Vision
- Wisdom

These are the characteristics that those who have been delivered from double-mindedness need in order to rebuild their true personalities, their godly personalities. They must have time to develop their real personalities while they are receiving deliverance. It is important to be led by the Holy Spirit when ministering, because there are varying degrees of demonization in different people.

ACCEPTANCE IN THE BELOVED

Since rejection is such a common problem, and since it is the core of double-mindedness, it is no wonder that it is mentioned as part of the redemption story of Christ. Jesus was rejected so that we could be delivered from rejection. Isaiah 53:3 tells us that He was despised and rejected of men. He was rejected by the high priests and the Pharisees. Why did Jesus go through rejection as one of the major areas in His passion? Because man needs to be delivered from rejection. He took upon Himself our rejection so that He could deliver us from rejection. The biggest rejection came when He asked, "My God, My God, why have You forsaken Me?" (Matt. 27:46), because at that moment He became sin, and His Father rejected Him. God always rejects sin. Jesus became sin, went through rejection, suffered, and was beaten, wounded, and bruised in order to deliver us from rejection.

Rejection is the open door to the double-minded personality, and a major aspect of deliverance and salvation. And now, because of Christ's rejection, we are accepted in the Beloved (Eph. 1:4–6). We are accepted through the blood of Jesus. We are accepted by grace. We don't have to be perfected through legalism or keeping laws. We can be accepted by faith. This is the tremendous blessing of Christianity.

DELIVERANCE FROM DOUBLE-MINDEDNESS TAKES TIME

> Deliverance from the schizo personality takes time because the real self has often not developed very much at that point. If one is to be successful, he needs Jesus. Jesus will help the real person to develop. Obedience to Jesus' instructions are necessary. Bible study and prayer are needed.[1]

The development of the real person has been hindered by demons and needs to be developed as the person receives deliverance. This development takes time. Many people would be shocked to discover that much of their personality is false and their "real" personality is underdeveloped. The deliverance is "little by little." As Frank Hammond said, "So much of the personality of the schizophrenic is not his real self but a nest of demonic behaviors that have flourished and been cultivated from the birth of rejection within the individual. As deliverance beings, the 'real self' must have Jesus, and He must begin to form His personality in them. Deliverance is the only answer for the schizophrenic."[2]

> I will not drive them out before you in one year, lest the land become desolate and the beasts of the field multiply against you. Little by little I will drive them out before you, until you become fruitful and inherit the land.
> —EXODUS 23:29–30

Israel had to grow in order to possess the land of Canaan. They were not large enough as a nation to possess it immediately. God promised to drive the enemy out "by little and little."

This principle applies to the double-minded deliverance. The cluster of demons in the rejection stronghold must be separated from the cluster of demons in the rebellion stronghold and over time cast out.

The following list shows how the demons in rejection link up with the demons in rebellion.

- Rejection spirits: Lust, fantasy, perversion, jealousy, paranoia, self-pity, depression, suicide, guilt, pride, vanity, loneliness, fear, attention seeking, inferiority, harlotry, rejection, unfairness, withdrawal, fantasy, daydreaming, timidity, self-awareness, shyness, sensitivity, chattering, nervousness, vivid imaginations, fear of germs, frustration, impatience, inordinate affection for animals, intolerance, insanity, self-rejection, self-accusation, tension, fear of people, compulsive confession, envy, fear of judgment, false compassion, fear of rejection, false responsibility, despondency, despair, discouragement, hopelessness, condemnation, unworthiness, shame, perfection, and ego.

- Rebellion spirits: Fear, accusation, rebellion, pride, disobedience, selfishness, hatred, resentment, violence, murder, memory recall loss, paranoia, suspicion, distrust, confrontation, self-will, stubbornness, anger, root of bitterness, judgment, self-deception, self-delusion, self-destruction, unteachableness, control, possessiveness, unforgiveness, retaliation, false beliefs, disrespect of authority, and antisubmissiveness.

DEMONIC CLUSTERS

Double-mindedness, from the standpoint of demonic problems, occurs when two or more demons in a person get so strong that they attract their own cluster of demons; thus a personality in the person is developed by a demon cluster—for example, the perfectionistic, performance-driven personality.

Most of these clusters are headed by rebellion in one group and rejection in the other. These strong demons that wreak havoc on people's lives cause a disintegration of the development of the person's real personality, create distortions and disturbances in his life and relationships, cause the person to live or desire a secret life, and force him to build walls.

Rebellion allows the secret other self or selves to express another or other personalities:[3]

- Rejection: prenatal rejection, rejection in the womb, rejection after birth, self-rejection, fear of rejection, inability to give or receive love, starved for love

- Rebellion (rejection and rebellion are the core, the two main personalities): self-will, selfishness, stubbornness, disobedience, antisubmissiveness, aggression, unteachable

- Root of bitterness (three main areas are rejection, rebellion, and bitterness): resentment, bitterness, unforgiveness, hatred, violence, temper, anger, retaliation, murder, memory recall

- Double-mindedness (schizophrenia or double-mindedness are controls): hesitating, dubious, irresolute, unstable, unreliable, uncertain, unrealistic

- Paranoia (strong area; paranoid schizophrenic; rooted in fear): jealousy, envy, suspicion, distrust, persecution, fears, confrontation, many voices, insensitive, confrontation with honesty at all costs, delusions, false grandeur, omnipotence, false beliefs

- Mental illness (schizophrenia; paranoia; mental illness): insanity, madness, mania, retardation, senility, hallucinations

- Self (the schizophrenic is constantly looking at self): self-pity (fear of judgement, insecurity, inferiority); self-accusation (compulsive confession, self-hatred, self-unforgiveness); self-condemnation (attention seeking); self-will (selfishness, stubbornness); self-deception (self-delusion, self-seduction, pride, unteachableness); self-awareness (timidity, shyness, loneliness, sensitiveness)

- Lust (weds a person to the world for love): fantasy lust, harlotry, perverseness, sexual impurity, false compassion, false love

- Depression (the devil's d's: rejection to depression to suicide): despondency, despair, discouragement, defeatism, defective, helplessness, hopelessness, suicide, death, insomnia, morbidity, false spirits

- Fears (paranoia; phobias; fears): people, mental insanity, germs, hysteria, phobias

- Control (demonic control of others: parents, mates, pastors, etc.): domination, witchcraft, possessiveness, conniving, manipulation

- Indecision (double-mindedness; indecision): procrastination, compromise, confusion, forgetfulness, indifference, apathy

- Unfairness (no one treats them fairly): withdrawal, fantasy, daydreaming, unreality, vivid imagination, pouting, pretension

- Talkativeness (cannot let others talk): nervousness, tension

- Accusation toward other (keeps one from looking at self): projection, criticism, faultfinding, judgementalism

- False compassion (false concern for others; false spiritual gifts): false responsibility, false burden, false love, inordinate affection for animals

- Guilt (demonic prolonged false emotions): condemnation, unworthiness, shame, embarrassment

- Perfection (an effort to earn respect and acceptance of others): intolerance, pride, irritability, vanity, frustration, anger, ego, impatience, criticism

LOOSE YOURSELF FROM DOUBLE-MINDEDNESS

Shake yourself from the dust; arise, O captive Jerusalem. Loose yourself from the bonds of your neck, O captive daughter of Zion.

—ISAIAH 52:2

This is a prophetic word to believers everywhere. We have been given the power and authority to loose ourselves from all types of bondage. Synonyms for the word *loose* include disjoin, divorce, separate, asunder, sever, unhitch, disconnect, detach, unseat, unbind, unchain, unfetter, unloose, free, release, liberate, break up, break in pieces, smash, shatter, splinter, demolish, force apart. This is the strategy for deliverance from double-mindedness as mentioned about. The two—rejection and rebellion—must be loosed from each other and then loosed from you. The word *loosed* also means to forgive or pardon.

Zion is a prophetic word and symbol for the church. Isaiah prophesied that Zion would be a "captive daughter." This is so true of the condition of the church today. Even though many are saved and have received the promise of the Spirit, there are still many bondages that remain in the lives of believers. But we have been given a prophetic promise and a command to loose ourselves. Jesus told His disciples that "whatsoever" we loose on earth is loosed in heaven (Matt. 18:18, KJV). In other words, you can loose whatsoever is binding, harassing, or operating in your life contrary to the will of God because you have been given the authority to do so.

Throughout this book we have discussed a range of demonic manifestations operating within double-mindedness. Now that we have identified the enemy, we can proceed to free ourselves from his clutches.

THE TRUTH ABOUT SELF-DELIVERANCE

The question is often asked of me, "Can a person deliver himself of demons?" My answer is yes, and it is my conviction that a person cannot really keep himself free of demons until he walks in this dimension of deliverance.

How is it that a person can deliver himself? As a believer (and that is our assumption), he has the same authority as the believer who serves in deliverance ministry. He has the authority in the name of Jesus! And Jesus plainly promised those who believe, "In my name shall they cast out devils" (Mark 16:17, kjv).

Usually a person needs only to learn how to go about self-deliverance. After a person has experienced an initial deliverance at the hands of an experienced minister, he can begin to practice self-deliverance.[4]

One of the greatest revelations is the revelation of self-deliverance. We can loose ourselves from any control of darkness (Isa. 52:2). We can exercise power and authority for our own lives. Jesus told us to cast out the beam from our own eye (Luke 6:42). The word used for *cast out* is the same word used in reference to casting out demons (*ekballō*).

After you have received deliverance through the ministry of other experienced deliverance ministers, you can practice self-deliverance. This is important. Take spiritual responsibility for your life. Don't depend on anyone else for your spiritual well-being. Confess the Word over your life. Pray strong prayers that rout the enemy. Do not allow self-pity to hold you back. Stir yourself up to prayer. This is a key to an overcoming life.

Those who experienced deliverance either came or were brought to Jesus. Someone had to take the initiative. It all begins with a decision. You cannot allow passivity to rob you of deliverance. You must open your mouth. Your deliverance is as close as your mouth.

There are many people frustrated with life. People who struggle can become overwhelmed by doubt and failure. Some are battling stress and pressure that often lead to emotional and physical problems. Jesus spent a considerable amount of time ministering to the oppressed. Multitudes came to hear Him in order to be healed and delivered from evil spirits.

Deliverance is the children's bread. Every child of God has a right to enjoy the benefits of deliverance. Deliverance brings freedom and joy. We have seen thousands of believers set free from demons through authoritative prayer.

Deliverance is a miracle ministry. You will see multiplied miracles through warfare prayer. The breakthroughs you will see are supernatural. Healings will multiply. Long-term bondages will be destroyed. Hidden roots will be exposed and eliminated. Inexplicable problems will be solved. Stubborn obstacles will be removed. Cycles of failure will be broken. Frustration and despair will be eliminated through warfare prayer. Discouragement and disappointment will be overcome.

The puzzling problems of life will be taken away. Lasting peace can finally be experienced. The abundant life can be enjoyed.

Failures that cause bitterness are reversed through warfare prayer. Prosperity and success will come. Advancement will be seen in different areas of your life. You will experience success in relationships, finances, ministry, and projects.

Deliverance is designed to eliminate the spiritual obstacles that impede progress. Deliverance makes the rough places smooth and the crooked places straight. You can see the enemy routed from your life. You can live free from the bondages and oppressions of demons. You can experience victory through prayer. Your words and prayers have tremendous power to destroy the works of darkness. Those who experience deliverance and release will see notable changes.

Sometimes the change is progressive, and sometimes it is instantaneous. It will, however, be dramatic. There will be an increase of joy, liberty, peace, and success. This will result in a better spiritual life with an increase of strength and holiness.

If we want to see breakthrough, we need to be patient. God promised Israel that He would drive the enemy out little by little (Deut. 7:22; Exod. 23:29–30). Unless you understand this principle, you will become weary in praying for some people, and you will become discouraged in your own deliverance. The more freedom you receive, the more you need to grow and possess your land.

You have the authority to bind and loose (Matt. 18:18). Webster's Dictionary defines the word *bind*, "to make secure by tying; to confine, restrain, or restrict as if with bonds...to constrain with legal authority...to exert a restraining or compelling effect."[5] It also means to arrest, apprehend, handcuff, lead captive, take charge of, lock up, restrain, check, or put a stop to.

Binding is done by legal authority. We have legal authority in the name of Jesus to bind the works of darkness; this encompasses sin, iniquity, perversion, sickness, disease, infirmity, death, destruction, curses, witchcraft, sorcery, divination, poverty, lack, strife, lust, pride, rebellion, fear, torment, and confusion. We have legal authority to put a stop to these things in our lives and in the lives of those to whom we minister.

Loose means to untie, to free from restraint, to detach, to disjoin, divorce, separate, unhitch, get free, get loose, escape, break away, unbind, unchain, unfetter, free, release, unlock, liberate, disconnect, and forgive. People need to be loosed from curses, evil inheritance, familiar spirits, sin, guilt, shame, condemnation, control, domination, manipulation, intimidation, mind control, religious control, sickness, disease, deception, false teaching, sin, habits, worldliness, carnality, demons, tradition, ungodly soul ties, ungodly pledges, ungodly vows, spoken words, hexes, vexes, jinxes, trauma, and cults. We have legal authority in the name of Jesus to loose ourselves and others to whom we minister from these destroying influences.

> Deliver yourself as a doe from the hand of the hunter, and as a bird from the hand of the fowler.
> —PROVERBS 6:5

> Deliver yourself, O Zion, you who live with the daughter of Babylon.
> —ZECHARIAH 2:7

WHAT WILL KEEP YOU FROM RECEIVING DELIVERANCE AND BREAKTHROUGH?

There are times when people want to skip right to the binding and loosing, casting out and loud praying, wanting to command the enemy in the name of Jesus to do this or that and go here or there. But there will be no deliverance while the enemy has full reign in a person's life. You must renounce and put to an end to the following things if you want to see real and lasting freedom, deliverance, and breakthrough in your life.

1. Curses
2. Sin
3. Pride
4. Passivity
5. Ungodly soul ties
6. Occultism
7. Fear
8. Embarrassment
9. Unbelief
10. Lack of desire
11. Unforgiveness
12. Lack of knowledge

With any of these twelve things actively operating in your life, you will find yourself in a cycle of bondage, not ever receiving complete freedom. Any of these things give demonic powers legal and biblical grounds to remain in your life and wreak havoc. These legal grounds must be destroyed in order to receive and maintain deliverance. We will address this in the next section.

Self-deliverance has limitations. We sometimes do not see as clearly for our own lives as we need to. People who are highly troubled will need to seek help from an experienced deliverance minister. Others can usually be more objective in discerning the problem, and also join their faith with yours for breakthrough.

If a person has serious bondages such as perversion, schizophrenia, occult involvement, and deep depression, then he or she may need the assistance of other believers. Shame will often keep a person from seeking outside help; those who operate in surrender to the Spirit of God regarding your deliverance will not be judgmental and will move in love and compassion.

There is no substitute for being in a strong local church, where a person is loved unconditionally. Now let's get delivered.

Loose Yourself From the Past

I have ministered to many believers who are still bound and tied to their pasts. The past can be a chain that keeps you from enjoying the present and being successful in the future.

While ministering deliverance to a young man, I encountered a strong spirit dwelling in him who boasted that he would not depart. I commanded the spirit to identify himself, and he replied that his name was Past. The spirit proceeded to explain that it was his job to keep the young man bound to his past so that he could not be successful in his Christian walk. The young man had been through a divorce, and his past continued to haunt him.

This encounter helped to give me a revelation of the fact that there are numerous spirits assigned to keep people bound to the past, leaving scars and wounds that have not completely healed. Many of these wounds have been infected and have become the dwelling places of unclean spirits.

People need to be loosed not only from demons but also from other people. Ungodly soul ties are avenues that spirits of control and manipulation utilize when working upon their unwary victims. Let's look at some of the things that could cause spirits to attach themselves to people who have had traumatic experiences in their past. For the purposes of clarity, we find the word *trauma* defined by Webster's as "a disordered psychic or behavioral state resulting from severe mental or emotional stress or physical injury."[6]

Traumatic experiences can open the door for demons. These can and often include accidents. Mentioned below are two such traumatic experiences that greatly affect the lives of individuals.

Rape

> They ravished [raped] the women in Zion, the virgins in the cities of Judah.
> —LAMENTATIONS 5:11

Rape is one of the most traumatic experiences a person can have. It is a violation that leaves deep scars in the psyche of the person who is victimized by this ungodly act. The door is opened for a host of evil spirits to enter and operate throughout the life of the victim.

Spirits of hurt, distrust, lust, perversion, anger, hatred, rage, bitterness, shame, guilt, and fear—all manifestations of the rejection side of the double-mindedness spirit—can enter and torment the person for the rest of her life if not discerned and cast out. Rape can also be a curse, and there is often a history of this sin in the bloodline.

Rape has always been in the history of oppressed people. It was (and is) common for victors to rape the women of the vanquished. It is one of the most shameful and humiliating acts that can be perpetrated upon an oppressed people.

Often victims of rape carry sexual blockages into marriage, including spirits of frigidity, bound and blocked emotions, hatred of men, and fear of sexual intercourse. Individuals can grow up with deep roots of bitterness that poison the system, opening the door for spirits of sickness and infirmity, including cancer, as we saw in chapter 7.

If you have experienced any kind of sexual trauma like rape or molestation, pray this prayer and allow the Holy Spirit to begin to make you whole again:

> *Father, in Jesus's name I loose myself from this prowling demon that sought to steal, kill, and destroy my body, my sexuality, and my worth. I loose myself from any hatred, bitterness, and unforgiveness. I loose myself from blaming myself for this violation. I loose myself from any soul ties, spirits of infirmity, or other evil spirits that would seek to latch on to my life because of this trauma. I loose myself from any bondages that would keep me from experiencing healthy and free marital intimacy. Amen.*

Incest

Another common sexual violation is the sin of incest. Incest can also result from a curse, and there can be a history of this sin in the bloodline. It is an act that causes much shame and guilt. It opens the door for all kinds of curses, including insanity, death, destruction, confusion, perversion, and sickness. Often the victim blames himself for this act even though it may have been the result of a seducing spirit. If this is something that the enemy has oppressed you with, begin praying this prayer for deliverance and healing:

Father, in Jesus's name I loose myself from the shame, guilt, soul ties, and any other hindering spirit that would try to keep me from living a whole and healthy life. I loose myself from the painful memories of this abuse and declare that I am washed clean, inside and out. I loose myself from every demonic spirit that would seek to enter through this open door, and I shut this door to my past and pray a hedge of protection around my future. Amen.

Loose Yourself From Ungodly Soul Ties

Cursed be their anger, for it is fierce; and their wrath, for it is cruel! I will divide them in Jacob and scatter them in Israel.

—GENESIS 49:7

The Lord separated Simeon and Levi because they exerted bad influence upon one another. A soul tie is a bond between two individuals; the souls (minds, wills, emotions) of individuals knit or joined together. Ungodly soul ties can be formed through fornication (Gen. 34:2–3) and witchcraft (Gal. 3:1; 4:17).

As mentioned earlier, people need to be loosed not only from demons but also from other people. Ungodly soul ties are avenues through which spirits of control, domination, witchcraft, and manipulation operate. If you are linked with the wrong people, you will be in bondage, often unknowingly.

It is never the will of God for one individual to control another. True freedom is being delivered from any controlling power that hinders you from fulfilling the will of God. Often those under control are unaware that they are being controlled. This is why many times the control is so difficult to break.

An ungodly soul tie will result in the presence of an evil influence in your life. While good soul ties help you in your walk with God, ungodly soul ties hinder you in your walk with the Lord. Ungodly soul ties in the Bible include the ties between Ahab and Jezebel (1 Kings 18); Solomon and his wives, who turned his heart away from the Lord (1 Kings 11:1–4); and Levi and Simeon (Gen. 49:5–7).

> *Father, in Jesus's name I loose myself from all relationships that are not ordained of God. All relationships that are not of the Spirit but of the flesh. All relationship based on control, domination, or manipulation. All relationships based on lust and deception. Amen.*

LOOSE YOURSELF FROM THE MEMORY OF PAST EXPERIENCES

Forgetting those things which are behind...
—PHILIPPIANS 3:13

There is an evil spirit named *memory recall* that can cause a person to have flashbacks of past experiences. This keeps a person in bondage to traumatic experiences of the past. This spirit causes a person to remember experiences of hurt, pain, and rejection. Although there may be experiences in your life you will never completely forget, you should not be in bondage to the past through your memory.

The enemy should not be able to trigger things in your memory that hinder you in your present or future life. This is why your memory needs to be loosed from bad experiences of hurt and trauma. Pray now:

Father, in Jesus's name I loose myself from the effects of all the bad memories, painful memories, and memories of the past that would hinder me in the present or future. Amen.

Loose Yourself From Unforgiveness and Bitterness

Unforgiveness opens the door for tormenting spirits (Matt. 18). Bitterness opens the door for spirits of infirmity, including arthritis and cancer. It is symbolized by gall and wormwood. Unforgiveness is the result of being hurt, rejected, abandoned, disappointed, abused, raped, molested, taken advantage of, lied about, cheated, talked about, and so forth.

Father, in Jesus's name I loose myself from all bitterness, unforgiveness, and resentment. I loose to God those who have offended me or hurt me in any way. I loose myself from all spirits of infirmity that have entered as a result of my bitterness. I close that door, in Jesus's name. Amen.

LOOSE YOURSELF FROM EMOTIONAL
PAIN AND BONDAGE

Are you loosed in your emotions? The emotions are a part of the soul along with the will and the mind. There are many people bound and blocked in their emotions. Spirits of hurt, rejection, anger, a broken heart, grief, sadness, hatred, bitterness, and rage can occupy the emotions, causing emotional pain.

Your emotions were created by God to express joy and sorrow. Both should be natural responses to different situations. The enemy, however, comes in to cause extremes in the emotional realm, including blockage, whereby a person is unable to express the proper emotions.

Emotional pain and bondage can come as a result of traumatic experiences of the past, including rape, incest, abuse, death of a loved one, war, tragedies, rejection, abandonment, accidents, etc. If you need deliverance to be able to express or control your emotions in a godly way, use this prayer to begin the rebuilding process:

> In the name of the Lord Jesus Christ, by the authority given to me to bind and loose, I loose my emotions from every evil spirit that has come in as a result of experiences of the past. I loose myself from all hurt, deep hurt, pain, sadness, grief, anger, hatred, rage, bitterness, fear, and bound and blocked emotions. I command these spirits to come out, and I decree freedom to my emotions in the name of the Lord Jesus Christ. Amen.

Loose Yourself From Occult Bondage

The word *occult* means "hidden." Involvement in the occult opens the door for many demons, including spirits of depression, suicide, death, destruction, sickness, mental illness, addiction, lust, etc. Involvement in the occult is related to witchcraft, a demonic spirit that can be traced back to the root spirit of rebellion. Jezebel is picture of this manifestation. Occult practices include the following:

- Ouija board
- Palm reading
- Psychic readings
- Drugs (from the Greek word *pharmakeia*, meaning "sorcery"[7])
- White magic
- Horoscopes
- Tea leaf reading
- Readers and advisers
- Black magic
- ESP

Father, in Jesus's name I loose myself from all occult involvement; all sorcery, divination, witchcraft, psychic inheritance, and rebellion; all confusion, sickness, death, and destruction as a result of occult involvement. Amen.

Loose Yourself From Mental Attacks

For as he thinks in his heart, so is he.
—Proverbs 23:7

The way that you think determines who you are. The mind has always been a favorite target of the enemy. If the devil can control your mind, he can control your life. Spirits that attack the mind include mind control, confusion, mental breakdown, mind-binding and mind-binding spirits, insanity, madness, mania, fantasy, evil thinking, migraines, mental pain, and negative thinking. These are what I call "stinking thinking."

The good news is that you can loose yourself (including your mind) from all evil influences that operate through your mind. Mind control is a common spirit that has been identified by the name *octopus*. Mind-control spirits can resemble an octopus or squid with tentacles that grasp and control the mind. Deliverance from mind control releases a person from mental pressure, mental pain, confusion, and mental torment. Mind-control spirits can enter through listening to ungodly music, reading occult books, pornography, false teaching, false religions, drugs, and passivity.

In Jesus's name I loose my mind from all spirits of control, confusion, mental bondage, insanity, madness, fantasy, passivity, intellectualism, knowledge block, ignorance, mind-binding, lust, and evil thinking. Amen.

LOOSE YOURSELF FROM A DEMONICALLY CONTROLLED WILL

Not My will, but Yours, be done.
—LUKE 22:42

One of the greatest gifts given to man is that of a *free will*. The freedom to choose and to decide is given to everyone. The Lord does not force us to obey Him. He gives us the choice to humble ourselves and submit our will to His will.

The devil, on the other hand, attempts to dominate and control our will for his evil purposes. When you find yourself unable to submit your will to the will of God, it is because your will is being controlled by the powers of darkness. Your will needs to be *loosed* to follow the will of the Lord. Spirits that invade and control the will include stubbornness, self-will, antisubmissiveness, rebellion, pride, disobedience, lust, and witchcraft.

> *Father, in Jesus's name I loose my will from all control, domination, and manipulation from Satan, his demons, and other people. I loose my will from all lust, rebellion, stubbornness, pride, self-will, selfishness, and antisubmissive spirits that block and hinder my will. I break and loose myself from all chains around my will, and I submit my will to the will of God. Amen.*

LOOSE YOURSELF FROM SEXUAL PERVERSION

Escape from sexual immorality…
—1 CORINTHIANS 6:18

Lust is a spirit that is pervasive in our day and age. Sexual perversion includes incest, homosexuality, lesbianism, masturbation, pornography, fornication, and adultery. The sex drive is one of the strongest appetites in the human body. Satan desires to control and pervert it outside the marital relationship in which it is blessed.

Many believers struggle in this area with the companion spirits of guilt and condemnation. Spirits of lust and perversion can operate in any part of the physical body, including the genitals, hands, eyes, mouth, stomach, and so on. Any part of the body given to sexual sin will be invaded and controlled by spirits of lust. (An example would be the eyes in viewing pornography, the hands in acts of masturbation, or the tongue in filthy conversation.)

> *In the name of Jesus, I loose all members of my body—including my mind, memory, eyes, ears, tongue, hands, feet, and my entire sexual character—from all lust, perversion, sexual impurity, uncleanness, lasciviousness, promiscuity, pornography, fornication, homosexuality, fantasy, filthiness, burning passion, and uncontrollable sex drive. Amen.*

LOOSE YOURSELF FROM EVIL INHERITANCE

Weaknesses and tendencies can be inherited from the sins of the fathers. For example, a person born to alcoholic parents will have a higher chance of becoming an alcoholic. Sicknesses and diseases can run in the bloodline, which is why doctors will often check to see if a person has a history of certain sicknesses in his or her family. Some of these evil inheritances include lust, perversion, witchcraft, pride, rebellion, divorce, alcohol, hatred, bitterness, idolatry, poverty, ignorance, and sicknesses (including heart disease, cancer, diabetes, and high blood pressure).

Familiar spirits are demons familiar with a person and the family. Often these spirits have been in the family for generations. Sometimes these spirits are difficult to break because their roots run deep into the family line.

> *In the name of Jesus, I loose myself from all evil inheritance, including inherited weaknesses, attitudes,*

thought patterns, sickness, witchcraft, lust, rebellion, poverty, ungodly lifestyles, and strife. Amen.

LOOSE YOURSELF FROM FEAR

Fear is a paralyzing spirit that keeps people bound in many areas of their lives. This spirit manifests itself in numerous ways: fear of rejection (works with rejection and self-rejection), fear of hurt, fear of authority (including pastors), fear of witchcraft, fear of career, fear of dying, fear of failure, fear of the future, fear of responsibility, fear of darkness, fear of being alone, fear of what people think of you, fear of what people say about you, fear of hell, fear of demons and deliverance, fear of poverty, terror, fright, sudden fear, apprehension. All of these manifestations must be broken in the name of Jesus.

In the name of Jesus, I loose myself from all fears, including childhood fears, fears from trauma, fears from the past, and all inherited fears. Amen.

LOOSE YOURSELF FROM REJECTION

Rejection prevents one from giving or receiving love from God or from other people. There is also a spirit called *rejection from the womb* that enters the womb because the child was unwanted. Self-rejection and fear of rejection are other related spirits. As we've already learned, rejection is also a doorkeeper. This spirit opens the door for other spirits to enter, including fear, hurt, unforgiveness, and bitterness. It links with rebellion, causing double-mindedness.

Almost everyone has experienced rejection at one time or another in life. People can be rejected because of their gender, skin color, economic status, size, shape, etc. Rejection is a major stronghold in the lives of many.

In the name of Jesus, I loose myself from the spirit of rejection. I am accepted in the Beloved. I am the chosen one of God in Christ Jesus. I loose myself from self-rejection and sabotage. I loose myself from fear of man and people-pleasing. I seek only to please God. I loose myself to receive love from God and from others without fear. I close the door on rejection, fear, hurt, unforgiveness, bitterness, and rebellion. In Jesus's name, I pray. Amen.

Loose Yourself From a Guilty Conscience

To be *loosed* means to be forgiven and pardoned. You have been forgiven by the Father through the blood of Jesus. You are loosed from guilt, shame, and condemnation. You must also be loosed from the law (legalism). The law brings condemnation and judgment, but Jesus brings forgiveness and reconciliation. We loose our conscience by applying *the blood of Jesus* by faith.

Satan uses guilt and condemnation to beat down the believers. Believers who don't understand grace struggle in their Christian lives, never measuring up to religious standards imposed upon them through legalism. To be free in your conscience is to have the peace of God rule in your mind and heart.

In the name of Jesus, I loose myself from all guilt, shame, condemnation, self-condemnation, and legalism. Amen.

WHAT TO EXPECT WHEN RECEIVING DELIVERANCE

While many deliverances involve obvious physical manifestations, not all react in this manner. Some spirits leave quietly and nonviolently. You may not have a strong physical reaction when receiving deliverance; therefore, don't be disappointed if you don't receive in this manner. What you should expect is a release. You know there is a release when

1. the oppressive force disappears;

2. heaviness lifts;

3. uneasiness goes away;

4. the burden or load lightens;

5. there is an inner sense of liberty, freedom, and divine satisfaction or contentment; and

6. the joy of the Lord comes, and you are able to rejoice.

The results of deliverance are righteousness, peace, and joy in the Holy Ghost (Rom. 14:17). When devils are cast out, the kingdom of God has come (Matt. 12:28).

How to Maintain Your Deliverance

Self-control is the main key to maintaining your deliverance. You must become vigilant in identifying and eradicating the areas of your life that were out of control. Do not go back to a lifestyle where you are easily carried away, disorderly, out of hand, rebellious, uncontrollable, ungovernable, unmanageable, unruly, or undisciplined. The Holy Spirit is your compass and magnifying glass in this area. An undisciplined lifestyle will bring you right back into bondage. There is no lasting deliverance and freedom without discipline.

> He who has no rule over his own spirit is like a city that is broken down and without walls.
> —Proverbs 25:28

The Contemporary English Version (CEV) translates Proverbs 25:28 like this: "A person without self-control is like a breached city, one with no walls." Cities without walls were open to invasion and attack from outside forces. A person without self-control is open for demons.

To maintain your deliverance, you need to have self-control in these areas:

1. Thinking—Philippians 4:8 says, "Finally, brethren, whatever things are true, whatever things are noble, whatever things are just, whatever things are pure, whatever things are lovely, whatever things are of good report, if there is any virtue and if there is anything praiseworthy—meditate on these things" (NKJV).

2. Appetites—Proverbs 23:2 says, "And put a knife to your throat, if you are a man given to appetite."

3. Speaking—Proverbs 25:28 says, "As a city open, and without compass of walls; so is a man that may not refrain his spirit in speaking. (Like a city that is open, and without any walls surrounding it, is a man who cannot refrain his own spirit from speaking)" (WYC).

4. Sexual character—1 Corinthians 9:27 says, "But I discipline my body and bring it into subjection, lest, when I have preached to others, I myself should become disqualified" (NKJV).

5. Emotions—Proverbs 15:13 says, "A merry heart makes a cheerful countenance, but by sorrow of the heart the spirit is broken" (NKJV).

6. Temper—Ecclesiastes 7:9 says, "Do not hasten in your spirit to be angry, for anger rests in the bosom of fools" (NKJV).

Here's how you gain and maintain self-control, and thereby maintain your freedom from bondage:

1. Read God's Word daily.

2. Find a group of Bible-believing people, preferably a church, and regularly meet with them for worship, study, and ministry.

3. Pray with the understanding and in tongues.

4. Place the blood of Jesus on yourself and your family.

5. Determine as nearly as you can which spirits have been cast out of you. Make a list, for Satan will try to recapture these areas.

6. The way demons gain reentry is through a lax, undisciplined thought life. The mind is the battlefield. You must cast down imaginations, and bring every thought into the obedience of Christ (2 Cor. 10:5).

7. Pray to the Father fervently, asking Him to make you alert, sober, and vigilant against wrong thoughts (1 Pet. 5:8–9).

8. The demons signal their approach to you when the old thought patterns you once had try to return. As soon as this happens, immediately rebuke them. As quickly as possible, state verbally that you refuse them.

9. You have the authority to loose the angels of the Lord to battle the demons (Heb. 1:14; Matt. 18:18). Bind the demons and loose upon them the spirits of destruction (1 Chron. 21:12), burning and judgment (Isa. 4:4), from the Lord Jesus Christ. Loose warrior angels upon the demons.

Let the Light of Christ Shine on You

Deliverance brings the light of Christ into the dark places of your soul. Demons thrive in darkness, but deliverance shines a bright light on them and causes them to be uncomfortable. They cannot dwell in places with too much light. The Bible says that whatever is hidden must come to light. (See Luke 8:17.) Demons may try to lie in wait for the perfect time to pop up and destroy your life when you least expect it, but they will not last long when Jesus begins to shine on your life.

It should be every believer's goal to allow the light of the Lord to shine in us, on us, and through us. When we are healed and set free to live God-honoring, stable lives, Jesus is truly seen in us. We will not be shaken by the storms of life. People will look at us and wonder why we stand unshakeable, levelheaded, and full of peace and wisdom when life gets hard. They will begin to wonder who is this God in whom we have placed our trust. What a testimony our lives will be!

Jesus is the light. We are the children of light. Walking in the light of the Lord means walking in wisdom, understanding, and revelation. This means you do not have to stumble in darkness, but can walk in God's direction and purpose for your life. Too many people live in darkness, without the light of the Lord. Darkness is ignorance, confusion, and death.

There will be light wherever Jesus is lifted and exalted. Light is glory. Light is life.

> For you were formerly darkness, but now you are light in the Lord. Walk as children of light.
> —Ephesians 5:8

You are all the sons of light and the sons of the day. We are not of the night nor of darkness.

—1 THESSALONIANS 5:5

For God, who commanded the light to shine out of darkness, has shone in our hearts to give the light of the knowledge of the glory of God in the face of Jesus Christ.

—2 CORINTHIANS 4:6

CHAPTER 9

CRY UNTO THE LORD

Prayers for Deliverance From Double-Mindedness

Then they cried unto the Lord in their trouble, and He
saved them out of their distress. He sent His word and healed
them and delivered them from their destruction.

—PSALM 107:19–20

PRAYER DEMOLISHES STRONGHOLDS. When we pray, we enforce the victory over Satan that was won at the Cross. We execute the judgments written against him through our prayers. We reinforce the fact that principalities and powers have been spoiled (Col. 2:15). This honor is given to all of the saints of God.

We are encouraged to call upon the Lord (Jer. 33:3). The Lord delights in our prayers, and He delights in answering our prayers. Before we call, He will answer (Isa. 65:24). The Lord's ears are open unto the prayers of the righteous (1 Pet. 3:12). The effectual fervent prayer of a righteous man avails much (James 5:16). We are told to pray without ceasing (1 Thess. 5:17).

Our God hears prayer. All flesh should come to Him in prayer (Ps. 65:2). All believers have similar challenges, and all believers can overcome these challenges through prayer. God is no respecter of persons. He is near to all who call upon Him (Ps. 145:19). The Lord will hear your supplication and receive your prayers (Ps. 6:9). Calling upon the Lord will bring salvation and deliverance from your enemies (Ps. 18:3). This has always been a key to deliverance. You can pray yourself out of any adverse situation. The Lord is your helper. God will not turn away your prayers (Ps. 66:20). God will not despise your prayers (Ps. 102:17). The prayers of the upright are God's delight (Prov. 15:8).

Our faith-filled prayers are keys to seeing miracles and breakthrough on a consistent basis. Whatever we ask in prayer, believing, we will receive (Matt. 21:22).

Here are prayers based on the three strongholds—rejection, rebellion, and the root of bitterness—and demon clusters we uncovered throughout this book that are all rooted in double-mindedness.

PRAYER FOR RENOUNCING THE SPIRITS OF REJECTION AND SELF-REJECTION

Heavenly Father, I believe that I have been fearfully and wonderfully made. Lord, You created me— spirit, soul, and body. Lord, You desire for me to be healthy in all areas of my life—my spirit, my soul, and my body. And so, Lord, I ask You to heal me and deliver me from any negative image I might have in my life—any self-rejection, self-hatred, guilt, shame, fear, unforgiveness, bitterness, and resentment that I might have in my heart toward my mother, my father, my siblings; any person who has hurt me, rejected me, abandoned me, taken advantage of me, that has caused me to reject or hate myself.

Lord, forgive me if I have spoken words against my own life—if I had a death wish, or if I have said things against my own self, I break the power of those words. Any negative words out of my mouth against my life, I break the power of those words. Any self-inflicted curses of death, sickness, or destruction; I break the power of those words. Any demons that have come into my life through hurt, rejection, or bad relationships, I renounce you. You cannot stay in my life.

I forgive myself for anything that I have done in the past that I was ashamed of. I renounce all shame, all guilt, in the name of Jesus. I accept myself. I believe that You created me for a purpose. I am Your creation, and I will not reject myself. You made me a certain way. I will not despise it.

So today I renounce all self-rejection and self-hatred; all guilt, shame, fear, bitterness, anger, and resentment in my life that is affecting my immune system, blood system, skeletal system, nervous system, and glandular system, in the name of Jesus; my muscular system; anything that is affecting my bowels, bones, joints, stomach, pancreas, kidneys, liver, spleen, intestines, throat, and every organ in my body; my heart, in the name of Jesus.

I command every spirit that would operate in my heart, intestines, belly, any organ of my body that would cause it not to function properly—I command you to come out of my life.

All spirits of sickness, infirmity, disease, death, premature death, and destruction—in the name of Jesus, I renounce you tonight, and I command you to leave. Any spirit affecting my blood, my blood sugar level, my blood pressure level—I renounce you in the name of Jesus.

All pain, swelling, infirmity, and rottenness in my bones, I command you to leave my body; any demon that dries my bones, in the name of Jesus; any demon that causes my blood to be unhealthy, in the name of Jesus; any demon that causes my body to attack itself and destroy itself, you cannot stay in my body. I command you to leave, in the name of Jesus. I command you to go by the power of God; by the anointing of Jesus Christ you cannot stay. I renounce and repent, and command you to leave in Jesus name.

DECLARATIONS FOR RECEIVING
DELIVERANCE FROM REJECTION

I declare that You have sanctified me with Your word; Your word over me is truth (John 17:17).

Lord, You are my light and my salvation. You are the strength of my life. I will not fear anything or anyone (Ps. 27:1).

I believe and receive what You have said about me.

Your truth sets me free from the spirit of rejection.

You have nailed my rejection to the cross. I am set free.

You were despised and rejected. You are acquainted with my grief and sorrow. But by Your stripes, I am healed of rejection (Isa. 53:3–5).

The Lord is with me. I will not be afraid. What can man do to me (Ps. 118:6)?

The lines have fallen to me in pleasant places; yes, I have a good inheritance (Ps 16:6).

I am blessed with all spiritual blessings in heavenly places in Christ (Eph. 1:3).

I have been chosen by God from the foundation of the world (Eph. 1:4).

I am holy and without blame (Eph. 1:4).

I have been adopted as Your child according to the good pleasure of Your will (Eph. 1:5).

I am accepted in the Beloved (Eph. 1:6).

I am redeemed through the blood of Jesus (Eph. 1:7).

I am an heir (Eph. 1:11).

I am seated in heavenly places in Christ Jesus (Eph. 2:6).

I am the workmanship of the Lord, created in Christ Jesus for good works (Eph. 2:10).

I am a fellow citizen with the saints and members of the household of God (Eph. 2:19).

I have been given exceedingly great and precious promises, that I may be a partaker of the divine nature of Christ (2 Pet. 1:4).

My inner man is strengthened with might by the Spirit of God (Eph. 3:16).

I am rooted and grounded in love (Eph. 3:17).

I am renewed in the spirit of my mind (Eph. 4:23).

I walk in love (Eph. 5:2).

I am filled with the Spirit of God (Eph. 5:18).

I am more than a conqueror (Rom. 8:37).

I am an overcomer by the blood of the Lamb (Rev. 12:11).

I am the righteousness of God in Christ Jesus (2 Cor. 5:21).

I am healed (1 Pet. 2:24).

The Son has set me free (John 8:36).

I am born of God; therefore, I am victorious (1 John 5:4).

PRAYER FOR RENOUNCING BITTERNESS

Father, in the name of Jesus, I thank You that I do not have to suffer from bitterness because of life's experiences. Lord, every person has dealt with something that could cause any one of us to hold on to bitterness and anger. But Lord, I will not allow bitterness to destroy my life. I will not allow any bitterness to come between my family members and me. I will not allow bitterness to come because of satanic attacks. I will not allow bitterness to come because of lust. I will not allow bitterness to come because of alcohol. I will not die with bitterness. I will not allow bitterness to come out of my lips. I will not allow bitterness to destroy my physical health.

I renounce all bitterness, unforgiveness, anger, hurt, and rage, in the name of Jesus. Father, I come against all spirits of unfairness—feelings that life has been unfair. I renounce the victim mentality and feelings of being cheated. I will walk in love, forgiveness, humility, compassion, and kindness, in the name of Jesus.

Thank You, Lord. Thank You for delivering me from the root of bitterness, and from hatred and anger. Jesus, You died to overcome bitterness. And even on the cross You said, "Father, forgive them for they know not what they do" (Luke 23:34). You did not allow bitterness to come into Your heart, even when You were being crucified. Lord, You overcame bitterness, and You overcame it for me.

Bitterness, you are defeated. Jesus defeated you on the cross. You have no right to be in my life. You have no place in my life, in Jesus's name. Amen.

PRAYER TO CAST OUT THE
DEMON OF BITTERNESS

Heavenly Father, I believe that Jesus is the Son of God. I believe that Jesus died on the cross for my sins. I believe that Jesus overcame every principality, every power, through His death on the cross. I believe that Jesus defeated bitterness, unforgiveness, resentment, anger, hatred, rage, wrath, and murder; in the name of Jesus, these demons are defeated. The love of God and the power of the blood defeat you. You have no place to operate in my life.

I will not be a bitter person. I will not allow bitterness to destroy me, to destroy my body. I am delivered from the spirits of bitterness. I renounce all bitterness, anger, hatred, murder, rage, retaliation, spite, and revenge, in the name of Jesus. I renounce all pain, misery, and frustration, in the name of Jesus I renounce all sickness, all lust. In the name of Jesus, I renounce all alcohol and all drugs.

In the name of Jesus, I break the power of bitterness. If there is any bitter root in my life, I command You, in the name of Jesus, to be plucked up from the root. I renounce all hurt, all broken-heartedness. I forgive any person who has hurt me, mistreated me, taken advantage of me, disappointed me, rejected me, stolen from me, or cheated me. I forgive them, and I bless them.

I forgive my relatives for anything they've done to hurt me or disappoint me. I love them, and I bless them. In the name of Jesus, I forgive any leader, pastor, or authority figure who has ever hurt me, disappointed me, rejected me, or taken advantage of me. I forgive them, and I bless them.

In Jesus's name I loose myself from all bitterness, all anger, all hatred, all rage, all murder, and command these demons to leave my body, leave my heart, leave my mind, and leave my mouth. In the name of Jesus, you cannot stay; you must depart. I cast you out. Every strongman; every stronghold of bitterness, resentment, unforgiveness, and root of bitterness, I drive you out in Jesus's name.

Prayer for Physical Healing From Infirmities Resulting From Bitterness and Unforgiveness

Heavenly Father, I thank You that You are a healer. I believe You are Jehovah Rapha, the Lord that heals me. I will not allow my past bad experiences to make me bitter. I will not allow the root of bitterness to develop in my life. Lord, I forgive any person in my past who has ever hurt me, disappointed me, rejected me, abandoned me, abused me, or taken advantage of me in any way. I ask You to forgive them, and I forgive them. I loose love upon them. I release myself from all bitterness, hurt, rejection, and pain from my past.

In the name of Jesus, I cut every cord between infirmity and bitterness in my life. I renounce all sicknesses, diseases, and allergies in the name of Jesus, and I pray for healing. Any cancer or arthritis, you cannot take root in my system. I renounce you and drive you out. Lord, I commit myself to being kind, loving, merciful, and courteous toward others. In the name of Jesus, I will walk in forgiveness. I will not be mean. I will not retaliate. I will not walk in spite or revenge. I will not be malicious, in the name of Jesus.

Father, I thank You that I am healed, whole, and delivered. And I command every demon of bitterness, unforgiveness, resentment, anger, murder, retaliation, revenge, and spite to leave my life, in the name of Jesus. All demons of rebellion and stubbornness, you must go. You cannot stay in my life. I will be healed of all bitterness and resentment, in the name of Jesus. Thank You, Lord, for healing and delivering me.

PRAYER TO RELEASE FORGIVENESS TO OTHERS

If there are specific people you know you need to forgive, you need to do that now. Bless them and release yourself from bitterness. Holding on to bitterness is not the will of God for your life. If God is bringing names of people to your mind, you need to forgive them now. You can fashion your own prayer or use the one here as a starting point to release all those whom you need to forgive.

> *Heavenly Father, in the name of Jesus I release* [name the person] *for* [name the offense(s)]. *I forgive them. Lord, I know that You have said that vengeance is Yours to repay. I put my trust in You to work in this person's life according to Your perfect and just ways.*
>
> *I release all feelings of hurt, anger, bitterness, resentment, judgment, retaliation, revenge, getting even, wishing for their demise, and anything else that I have held and wished against* [name of person]*'s future.*
>
> *Lord, heal my memory of the hurtful events. Heal my eyes and ears from what I may have seen or heard in error. Bring me to a place of love for this person. Let me come to a place where I can pray prayers of blessing for* [him or her], *even if it is from afar. You are my example of perfect love and forgiveness when You prayed for those who crucified You: "Father, forgive them for they know not what they do." Help me, God, to be like You.*
>
> *Lord, I ask that You will heal me in every area of my mind, body, and soul that has been affected by my lack of forgiveness. Restore to me what the forgiveness, bitterness, and resentment have stolen from me.*
>
> *I also ask that You will forgive me for trying to take matters concerning* [name of person] *into my own hands. They are Yours to chasten or bless. Whatever I have done to cause them harm in any way, I ask*

that You will forgive me and restore to them what has been lost. In Jesus's name, I pray. Amen.

PRAYERS TO BREAK THE SPIRIT OF DOUBLE-MINDEDNESS

I bind and rebuke every spirit that would attempt to distort, disturb, or disintegrate the development of my personality in the name of Jesus.

I break all curses of schizophrenia and double-mindedness on my family in the name of Jesus.

I bind and rebuke the spirit of double-mindedness in the name of Jesus (James 1:8).

I bind and take authority over the strongmen of rejection and rebellion, and separate them in the name of Jesus.

I bind and cast out the spirits of rejection, fear of rejection, and self-rejection in the name of Jesus.

I bind and cast out all spirits of lust, fantasy, harlotry, and perverseness in the name of Jesus.

I bind and cast out all spirits of insecurity and inferiority in the name of Jesus.

I bind and cast out all spirits of self-accusation and compulsive confession in the name of Jesus.

I bind and cast out all spirits of fear of judgment, self-pity, false compassion, and false responsibility in the name of Jesus.

I bind and cast out all spirits of depression, despondency, despair, discouragement, and hopelessness in the name of Jesus.

I bind and cast out all spirits of guilt, condemnation, unworthiness, and shame in the name of Jesus.

I bind and cast out all spirits of perfection, pride, vanity, ego, intolerance, frustration, and impatience in the name of Jesus.

I bind and cast out all spirits of unfairness, withdrawal, pouting, unreality, fantasy, daydreaming, and vivid imagination in the name of Jesus.

I bind and cast out all spirits of self-awareness, timidity, loneliness, and sensitivity in the name of Jesus.

I bind and cast out all spirits of talkativeness, nervousness, tension, and fear in the name of Jesus.

I bind and cast out all spirits of self-will, selfishness, and stubbornness in the name of Jesus.

I bind and cast out the spirit of accusation in the name of Jesus.

I bind and cast out all spirits of self-delusion, self-deception, and self-seduction in the name of Jesus.

I bind and cast out all spirits of judgment, pride, and unteachableness in the name of Jesus.

I bind and cast out all spirits of control and possessiveness in the name of Jesus.

I bind and cast out the root of bitterness in the name of Jesus.

I bind and cast out all spirits of hatred, resentment, violence, murder, unforgiveness, anger, and retaliation in the name of Jesus.

I bind and cast out spirits of paranoia, suspicion, distrust, persecution, confrontation, and fear in the name of Jesus.

CHAPTER 10

BECOME A PSALM 112 BELIEVER

A Picture of the Stable Man

Praise the LORD!
Blessed is the man who fears the LORD,
who delights greatly in His commandments.
His offspring shall be mighty in the land; the generation of the upright shall
be blessed. Wealth and riches shall be in his house,
and his righteousness endures forever. To the upright there arises light in
the darkness; he is gracious, and full of compassion, and righteous. A good
man shows generous favor, and lends; he will guide his affairs with justice.

Surely the righteous man shall not be moved; the righteous
shall be in everlasting remembrance. He shall not be afraid
of evil tidings; his heart is fixed, trusting in the LORD. His
heart is established; he shall not be afraid, until he

sees triumph upon his enemies. He has given away freely; he has given to the poor; his righteousness endures forever; his horn shall be exalted with honor.

—PSALM 112:1–9

PSALM 112 GIVES a picture of the stable, single-minded, steadfast man. It is the exact opposite of the double-minded, wavering man from James 1:8. The man who fears the Lord is gracious, full of compassion, and lends. His heart is fixed and established. He cannot be moved. He is uncompromisingly and consistently righteous. His righteousness endures forever.

This psalm provides the standard to which all stable believers should aspire. Becoming like the man of Psalm 112 should be our goal. This man is a type of Christ, and the characteristics or traits that this passage reveals cannot be achieved except in Christ. These verses reveal the key to being truly prosperous from the inside out—prosperous in the sense that God intends for all of His people.

When most churches teach on prosperity, they do not teach it from the sense of someone who is prosperous from within. The Bible says that we are to prosper even as our souls prosper. Prosperity is more than financial abundance or having a lot of money. You can have money and no prosperity. If your marriage and other relationships are messed up, your mind, body, and/or spirit is messed up, and you have no peace, then you are not prospering.

Prosperity is wholeness, peace, favor, and having a blessed life. Prosperity is shalom. I talk about the blessing of shalom in my Covenant Series (see a listing of these and other books in the resources section of this book). Shalom means you enjoy relationships—*healthy* relationships. You enjoy a healthy mind and body, and healthy finances. True prosperity is a result of prospering on the inside.

Anytime you are not prospering, don't look to blame anyone or anything else; look on the inside. Ask God to show you what is not stable in your life and in your heart.

> Examine me, O LORD, and test me; try my affections and my heart.
> —PSALM 26:2

> Search me, O God, and know my heart; try me, and know my concerns, and see if there is any rebellious way in me, and lead me in the ancient way.
> —PSALM 139:23–24

Ask God to show you if there is anything that you need to be healed of and delivered from so that what is on the inside can manifest on the outside.

> Beloved, I pray that all may go well with you and that you may be in good health, even as your soul is well.
> —3 JOHN 1:2

If you are not prosperous on the inside, then any outward prosperity you obtain will be destroyed. You cannot sustain outward prosperity without being inwardly stable. There are a lot of people who are trying to prosper financially, physically, and mentally. They work on their bodies by eating healthy and exercising. They work toward having peace and a sound mind. They want to prosper. They believe it is God's will for them to prosper. Yet it is amazing to me how many of these same people—those who prophesy, speak in tongues, cast out demons, are saved and born again, love the Lord, stay in the Word, are filled with the Holy Ghost, praise God, worship, and do everything that they are taught to do—are not still prospering in their health, in their minds, in their finances, or in their relationships. They're unhappy, unsatisfied, confused, and mixed up. They are not prospering.

The truth is our lives are direct results of what is in our hearts. If you study 2 Corinthians 9, where Paul is encouraging the church to give, notice he quotes from Psalm 112. The Psalm 112 man's giving is mentioned right after the text discusses the man's heart condition. The more I've studied doublemindedness, the more I realize it is not only about indecision, doubting, wavering, and inconsistency; it is also something that is characteristic of the wicked. It is not a good thing.

In the two places the letter of James talks about doublemindedness, the writer applies this word to someone who has something impure in his heart. In the Scriptures doubleminded people are equated with sinful, wicked people. Doublemindedness is not the characteristic of a godly person. The godly person's prosperity grants him the ability to give to the poor; this flows out of a heart that is godly, fears the Lord, delights greatly in His commandments, and is established and fixed. God wants this kind of life for us. We need to recognize that when God saves us, He uses deliverance to stabilize our lives.

If our lives are messed up, it is usually because our hearts are messed up. The Bible says, "Keep your heart with all diligence, for out of it are the issues of life" (Prov. 4:23). The heart, in spiritual terms, is more than your physical pump. Your heart is your mind or spirit. It is the center of your being, and out of the center of who you are flows the issues of life.

One of the worst things we can believe about ourselves or other people is that we have good hearts even though our lives are messed up. Have you ever been to the funeral of the neighborhood drug dealer, and the preacher or a family member says something like, "He sold drugs, he got shot to death at thirty-five, but he had a good heart." No, he didn't have a good heart. He may have done some good things—maybe he bought some kids some candy, and provided for the material needs of his family. But if he sold drugs, was involved in crime and all kinds of mess, and got shot to death at an early age, then he didn't have a good heart. If he had a good heart, his life would not have been that messed up.

We cannot keep operating under the false assumption that we all have good hearts when the fruit of our lives is not good. Yes, we may have good motives from time to time, but if we are living messed up lives then our hearts are not good. We need a change of heart.

Your heart controls what comes out in your life. It is important to make sure that your heart, soul, and mind are right. That's what deliverance is for: to restore your soul; to deal with things on the inside of you that cause your heart not to be right—things such as rejection, rebellion, fear, anger, lust, hatred, resentment, bitterness, unforgiveness, envy, paranoia, selfishness, and distrust. If those things are in your heart, they are going to affect the way you live, from relationships to lifestyle to prosperity. You will not prosper the way God wants you to prosper if you do not prosper on the inside first.

Let's look at Psalm 112 verse by verse and learn what makes up a stable, prosperous person from the inside out.

Verse 1—Blessed, Happy, and to Be Envied

> Praise the LORD! Blessed is the man who fears the LORD, who delights greatly in His commandments.

It starts with "blessed," which means, happy or to be envied.

Verse 2—Releases Blessing on the Next Generation

> His offspring shall be mighty in the land; the generation of the upright shall be blessed.

Godliness in a person's life releases blessing upon the next generation. If we want our children to be blessed, then we need to live this kind of lifestyle.

Verse 3—Financially Prosperous With More Than Enough

> Wealth and riches shall be in his house, and his righteousness endures forever.

Here is a man who is prosperous financially. He has more than enough. He is not struggling in his finances. He is living in the blessing of the Lord. The Bible says in Proverbs 10:22, "The blessing of the LORD makes rich, and He adds no sorrow with it." When you read Psalm 112, it gives insight into this man's character and heart. It helps us answer these questions: Why is this man blessed? Why are his children blessed? Why does this man walk in such a level of blessing? Is it accidental? Is it just for a few lucky people and not for others? Or is there something about this person's heart that causes him to prosper?

VERSE 4—GRACIOUS, COMPASSIONATE, AND RIGHTEOUS

To the upright there arises light in the darkness; he is gracious, and full of compassion, and righteous.

In his dealings with people, this man is not judgmental, legalistic, cruel, vindictive, or bitter. He is gracious, kind, and loving. (Even though it is written in masculine terms, women are also included here.) It goes on to say that he is not filled with bitterness. He is not angry or hateful. As we have studied so far, we know that there are three major roots or strongholds in the double-minded personality: rejection, rebellion, and the root of bitterness.

When a person is rejected by people very early in life, she becomes rebellious. Oftentimes when a child becomes very rebellious it is a cry for attention because she feels rejected. Also, when people have been rejected, they become bitter. They get hurt. No one likes to be rejected. Being rejected is one of the most painful things that can happen to you. You can say it doesn't bother you, but rejection will always bother you. Everyone wants to be accepted; no one likes to be rejected. So you may become bitter, angry, unforgiving, retaliatory, resentful, and hateful. When you get like that, you cannot be a gracious, kind, loving person.

So we find that the person in this verse is not bitter, angry, or resentful. He is gracious, full of compassion, gentle, and kind. You cannot be this way as a double-minded person. Your rejection, anger, rebellion, and bitterness will eventually come out.

We can see that clearly this person does not suffer from double-mindedness. He is not suffering/struggling from those clusters or patterns of demons. He is showing us how we prosper on the inside, so that we prosper on the outside.

VERSE 5—GENEROUS, LENDS, AND IS JUST

> A good man shows generous favor, and lends [not with the hope of return; he just gives—Job 29; read the Amplified Version]; he will guide his affairs with justice [discretion].

The Psalm 112 man has wisdom and discretion. He is a giver; he gives to the poor and hurting. You will find a correlation between the Psalm 112 man and Job before he suffered his losses in Job 29. Stable people are generous people.

VERSE 6—UNSHAKEABLE, IMMOVABLE, AND RIGHTEOUS FOREVER

> Surely the righteous man shall not be moved; the righteous shall be in everlasting remembrance.

The Psalm 112 man is uncompromisingly righteous. He does what is right all the time. There is no wavering. He doesn't do right sometimes, then at other times do wrong. For him doing right is not a struggle. When it comes to doing right or wrong, he doesn't have to make a decision; he has already decided that he will do right. When wrong things come up, he is not overwhelmed with the temptation, because he has already settled in his heart that he will do right.

The reason people struggle with temptation, can't overcome certain things, and always end up doing something wrong is because they have not settled in their hearts and made a decision that when right and wrong come up, there is no choice. The stable person, on the other hand, already knows she is going to choose to go the right way. She doesn't have to stand there and try to figure out which way she is going. She has already made the decision that she will stand for what is right and godly.

As a stable-minded believer, if you see something that doesn't belong to you and something says "steal it," to you that is not an option. You have already made a decision that you are not a thief. You do what is right. For consistent success in this area, you don't wait until the point of temptation to make a choice. You have already decided ahead of time to do what is right. It is settled, and your heart is so established (v. 8) that all you'll do is right. Like the Psalm 112 man, your righteousness can endure forever (v. 9).

The reason why I preach this so strongly is because I see so many who are up and down. They do well for a while, for a season, and then they backslide. As believers we should be looking to live a consistent lifestyle. Our righteousness should go on forever. Does your righteousness extend beyond a temporary time? Or are you double-minded?

Double-mindedness is not normal.

Sometimes we excuse the manifestations of double-mindedness as normal. We think that being inconsistent is natural and everyone is just like that. We accept it. But to be one way one minute and the total opposite another is not godly. People cannot trust that. When you are like that—a roller coaster of emotions, in and out of relationships, always in conflict or confusion—then you will not be able to prosper in life. There will be no joy or peace in those situations. That is not God.

We cannot compromise and settle for inconsistency in living according to the Word of God. Like the Psalm 112 man, our righteousness should continue on forever. This is your modus operandi as a believer—consistency and stability.

How many times are you going to "get saved"?

How many times are you going to come back to the Lord? How many times are you going to come to the altar? How many times are you going to be the prodigal son? How many times are you going to be in the pigpen? Where is your consistency with God? You can't be happy with a life like this. Once you know God and get out of fellowship, it's hard to be out of step with God. When you backslide, you deal with torment. You can't rest or be at peace because your heart has known the fellowship of God. What kind of life is that? You're tormented, vexed, scared…Who wants to live a life they can't enjoy? Jesus did not come and die so that you would have an up-and-down, drama-filled life. He came to provide a way for you to become stable in the Lord.

The Psalm 112 believer is unshakeable.

A double-minded person is easily moved. Things easily shake them. They are easily discouraged and depressed. When something comes up against them, they have a difficult time handling it. Many times their only recourse is to shut down and withdraw from everything and everybody, sometimes for weeks at a time. This is not to say that there aren't times when God leads you to come away from everything to pray and seek Him. But for double-minded people, it is more than this. They become shaken and messed up by the difficulties of life to the point that they cannot stand. They get wiped out. They stop coming to church and receiving or answering the calls and visits of concerned friends and family. They just get overtaken. These are the same people who just last week or last month were decreeing and declaring the Word, shouting, worshipping, and on fire for God. What happened? They don't have what used to be called "staying power." Something hits them, and they get moved—depressed, discouraged—and temporarily give up.

We all deal with life, but this behavior is not part of the personality of the Psalm 112 believer—the stable man. The Bible says that he shall not be moved—forever! What a powerful statement. This man is unmovable, unshakeable.

Now, understand that this is not about being so powerful that nothing fazes you. There are no super saints. But sometimes when you find yourself being moved, shaken, or filled with doubt, you may find yourself asking questions like

- Does God love me?

- Am I really saved?

- Am I going to make it?

- Does the Word really work?

- Did I really hear from God?

- Am I in the right church?

If you find yourself asking questions like these, then you have been shaken, and that is not good. It is not godly. It is not the characteristic of a Psalm 112 believer. The Bible says, "Be steadfast, unmovable, always abounding in the work of the Lord" (1 Cor. 15:58). Be consistent. Be unwavering.

Now I too have experienced heavy discouragement at various points in my thirty-plus years as a believer. At times, I didn't want to get up out of the bed. I slept all day and did not look forward to another day. What believer hasn't gone through that? We may feel that this isn't as bad or as sinful as what some others may do. We think, "Well, I'm not smoking, drinking, lying, cussing, fornicating…" Still, think about it: being completely knocked down by something in life is not the mark of a stable individual. That is a double-minded reaction to something that happens to you, something someone says to you or about you. One moment we're doing well; the next, something happens and we are thrown off. That is not stability. That is double-mindedness.

Of course we all struggle, but remember that is not the goal—just to get by and remain struggling; being on fire for God one minute and totally giving up and discouraged, living life like the wicked the next. Our goal is to become steadfast, unshakeable, single-minded, and fixed on God.

Verses 7–8—Unafraid, Fixed, and Established

> He shall not be afraid of evil tidings; his heart is fixed, trusting in the LORD. His heart is established; he shall not be afraid, until he sees triumph upon his enemies.

One of the main characteristics in the double-minded rejection personality is fear. The Psalm 112 believer is not a fearful person. We cannot prosper with fear in our lives. Fear immobilizes us and causes us to not do anything.

- Fear of rejection
- Fear of people
- Fear of confrontation
- Fear of God
- Fear of losing your salvation
- Fear of witchcraft
- Fear of being alone
- Fear of being raped
- Fear of getting married
- Fear of going broke
- Fear of not having enough
- Fear of not joining a church
- Fear of the pastor
- Fear of authority
- Fear of being hurt
- Fear of Jezebel
- Fear of failure
- Fear of going to hell
- Fear of demons
- Fear of animals
- Fear of thunder and lightning
- Fear of being robbed
- Fear of not getting married
- Fear of starving
- Fear of joining a church
- Fear of leaving a church
- Fear of leadership

There are so many fears by which we are bound. They are all a part of the rejection personality. God does not want us to be fearful people. When you are fearful, you withdraw, hide, and run because you don't want to be hurt or taken advantage of. Like a turtle, you go into a shell. Like an ostrich, you stick your head in the sand. You put up a shield and a defense. You don't want anyone to get close. You don't open up. You build up walls. You isolate yourself because you can't trust anyone.

That's not prosperity. Prosperity is having good relationships, not being a loner, not being isolated. The Bible says that the Psalm 112 believer is not afraid, because his heart is fixed, trusting in the Lord. He is not doubting, wavering, or struggling with unbelief. He trusts God. His heart is fixed on God.

This is the key to being stable-minded. If you go back to James 1:5–7, it says, "If any of you lacks wisdom, let him ask of God, who gives to all men liberally and without criticism, and it will be given to him. But let him ask in faith, without wavering. For he who wavers is like a wave of the sea, driven and tossed with the wind. Let not that man think that he will receive anything from the Lord." In other words, a wavering, double-minded person is a person who trusts God sometimes and other times he doubts, because his heart is not fixed. This goes back to being a heart issue.

The Psalm 112 believer's heart is established. She trusts in God, knowing He is her protector, deliverer, healer, and whatever else she needs. She doesn't have to worry about anything coming against her. "If God is for you, who can be against you?" (See Romans 8:31.) This believer is stabilized and confident not in himself but in God. This is how we should all want to live. We should not be tossed to and fro upon the waves of life.

A heart that is established is set, and as I said before, the decision to do the right thing has already been made in advance and cannot be changed or altered. The word *establish* brings to mind the foundation of a house, how it is set deep into the earth. When the winds and floods come, the house doesn't move or shake, because it has been established.

You cannot have a prosperous walk with God without being established and set. When you go in to get your physical heart checked, the technicians and the doctors are looking for a consistent heartbeat. Any irregularities are cause for concern. It could mean that you need any number of emergency medical interventions.

God is looking for the same thing: a consistent heartbeat for Him—joyful, peaceful, stable; righteous, holy, stable; kind, stable; compassionate, stable; merciful, stable; faithful, loyal, stable; loving, stable; consistent in your giving, worship, attendance, fellowship…month after month; year after year.

Can you say that about yourself? If not, you need deliverance. Healing and deliverance from the Lord can bring stability to your life. You cannot prosper without addressing this area of your life. Stability, steadfastness, and single-mindedness are the core and foundation of a prosperous believer's life. You cannot build anything else that will last without shoring up this area. The Bible says that a double-minded person is unstable in all his ways. This means he will not prosper long-term in anything without first becoming stable and fixed in his heart.

VERSE 9—GENEROUS

He has given away freely; he has given to the poor; his righteousness endures forever; his horn shall be exalted with honor.

God wants us to be consistent in our giving. Even believers go through difficult financial times. They may lose their jobs. They may come up against some other kind of financial roadblock. These are times where giving is challenging, and perhaps one may give less than he or she customarily does. This is not the kind of inconsistency I am referring to. I am referring to the kind of giving that is coerced, emotional, and is decided at a moment's notice. This kind of giving only occurs every now and then, and does not flow out of a heart that is fixed and established.

But the stable man is consistent in his giving. He is a regular giver. It is something that is a part of his righteous character, something he is fixed to do and has already established in his heart. He consistently supports the work of God. Never get out of the habit of giving; this is the characteristic of a righteous person.

Some people get angry or hurt by the church, so they stop giving. They don't like the message the pastor preaches, so they stop giving. There are people who backslide and stop giving. But this is not the practice of a consistent and stable person. He does not allow changes in life to shake him from doing what has already been set in his heart.

Some stop giving because of discouragement with their finances. They feel like God isn't answering their prayers for financial breakthrough. They've been declaring, "Money cometh," but nothing is changing. They question where the blessing of God is in their lives. They wonder why they always have a difficult time financially, with finding employment. When they do get some kind of overflow, something happens and all the overflow goes into repairing or recovering that situation. The car breaks down. The roof caves in. Unexpected illness occurs. But this is the reason why we are counseled to save money.

There was a time when I lent my car to my son, and somehow it broke down. We took it to the dealer, and they said the engine had locked up. We had a choice to either get a new engine or install a rebuilt one. The cost was $5,000. I could have blamed the devil, but this can happen when a car is not regularly serviced and the oil is not changed out regularly. I didn't go into deep depression over it. I didn't get angry at God. I went and got the money together and got the car fixed.

The reality is that things man builds can fall apart. God didn't make the car. Things like this happen in life. Everything is not the devil. Sometimes the refrigerator breaks down because it's old and it's time for a new one. Things break. No need to get the anointing oil and start rebuking devils. However, if this happens consistently, then you may have a spiritual problem.

But this kind of thing causes some people to want to stop giving. They become discouraged. Then giving gets even more difficult when they give to someone who is ungrateful or turns around and treats them badly. But the giving of stable, single-minded believers is not based on how people respond. They do what God tells them to do and give how He tells them to give, because they are not looking for man to bless them. They are looking to God to bless them. Jesus healed ten lepers, and only one came back to say thank you. He didn't get angry and take back the healing from the others who didn't show gratitude.

We do not give to get the praise of people. When we give, we give because we are being obedient to God. We do not give so someone will treat us right, or so they will like us more. They may never say thank you, but what you did to bless them is between you and God—just like how or if they show gratitude is between them and God.

You do not give in order to place someone in your debt. We are not here to control people. When you give to someone, release the gift. Let the person go on, and leave it between them and God how they live on from there—either filled with gratitude or not. This also means that you should be cautious about whom you accept things from. Some people hold gifts over other people's heads and always bring them up. They want to own others.

Regardless of how other people treat us, their actions should not determine our consistency in giving the way the Lord wants us to. Our hearts should be fixed. A person with a fixed heart is a giver. She will always be a giver—a cheerful giver. And no circumstance will change that. He knows that when he gives it will be given unto him, good measure, pressed down, and running over shall be poured into his bosom. (See Luke 6:38.)

It is more blessed to give than to receive! You must fix your heart in this area—just as you have to fix it in your heart that you are not going to be a fornicator. That is not a spur-of-the-moment decision you make when faced with a temptation. This is something you have already established in your heart long before the temptation crosses your path. This should be your pattern when it comes to giving and serving God in general.

THE PSALM 112 BELIEVER IS SINGLE-MINDED

There is a blessing to becoming single-minded. To be single-minded is to have one overriding purpose or goal, steadfast;

resolute, having but one aim or purpose; dedicated, firm in purpose or belief; characterized by firmness and determination.[1] *Single* in the Greek language is the *haplous*, which means "simple...whole, good fulfilling its office, sound, of the eye" (used in Matt. 6:22).[2] A single-minded personality is a whole or sound personality. It is whole and not divided. It is exclusively devoted to God and His Word. A single-minded person has a single heart. He or she is whole-hearted, committed, steadfast, and loyal. These are the characteristics or the trademarks of a stable believer.

> And continuing daily with one mind in the temple, and breaking bread from house to house, they ate their food with gladness and simplicity of heart.
>
> —ACTS 2:46

> Servants, obey those who are your masters according to the flesh, with fear and trembling, in sincerity of your heart, as to Christ.
>
> —EPHESIANS 6:5

> Servants, obey your masters in all things according to the flesh, serving not only when they are watching, as the servants of men, but in singleness of heart, fearing God.
>
> —COLOSSIANS 3:22

The opposite of this is double-mindedness, which often results in backsliding. In other words, having a single mind is a key to a person's relationship with God.

The Bible says, "Mark the perfect man, and behold the upright" (Ps. 37:37, KJV). This verse is saying, "Identify the perfect man, the mature man, the whole man." God tells us to mark him, put your finger on him. For the end of that man is peace (shalom)—prosperity, health, wealth, and favor. This is the result of a perfect man. When I say perfect, I don't mean a man who has never made a mistake. I mean a man who is whole and mature—a person who is stable, steadfast, and consistent.

If you can find five people in your life who are whole consistent and stable, that will be a miracle. Can you find five people whom you can say are complete, mature, consistent, righteous, godly, unchanging, not up and down or in and out, dependable, holy, consistently lovers of God, kind, and gracious? You will find a great number, if you can find five.

Many people *want* the blessing of Psalm 112. They *want* wealth and riches. They *want* prosperity. But they don't want to do what it takes to have their hearts purified so that they can first prosper on the inside. This should be the goal of every one of us. It's my goal. My prayer is, "Lord, do I line up with the Psalm 112 man?" I cannot say that consistently I've arrived, but I am closer than I was a few years ago. I'm growing. Being consistent and stable is my goal—to be consistent, gracious, kind, and loving; to have a heart that is not corrupted by demons; a heart that is not angry, bitter, lustful, or jealous; not full of rejection and hurt, selfishness, self-will, pride, accusation, and fear. Lord, I don't want any of that in me.

God wants consistent, stable people. Recognize that this is not something you do in your own strength. It comes by the grace of God and through deliverance. God stabilizes you. He fills you with the Holy Spirit. But when He does show you any inconsistency in your life, you need to deal with it. Don't ignore it.

Refuse to be a double-minded person. Do not allow double-mindedness in your life. You have access to God's power, grace, and deliverance. Exercise your faith. You can obtain the blessed life of Psalm 112. No matter what life throws at you, you can overcome it all and become a stable, unshakeable, and established believer through Christ.

Psalm 112 Declarations

Father I bless You. I thank You for prosperity. I believe in prosperity in my soul and in my life.

Lord, I ask You to prosper me on the inside that I might be prosperous on the outside. Thank You for making me whole.

Lord, I desire to have a heart that is fixed, one that is established, one that is stable and steadfast.

Lord, forgive me for any double-mindedness, any instability, any confusion I've allowed in my life.

Lord, I pray that You would heal me, deliver me, restore me, and make me whole.

I fall out of agreement with all double-mindedness. I loose myself from all rejection, all rebellion, all bitterness, and every spirit that is connected to double-mindedness; all lust, all fear, all depression, all discouragement, all inferiority, all pride, all stubbornness, all control, all paranoia, in the name of Jesus.

I loose myself from every false personality, every double-minded spirit, in the name of Jesus. I will not be this way. I loose myself in the name of Jesus.

Thank You, Lord, for delivering me and setting me free. I receive healing, restoration, and wholeness in my heart, mind, and soul.

Thank You, Lord, for uniting my heart. I will not have a divided heart. I will have a united heart to fear You all the days of my life. Thank You, Lord.

Let the blessings of Psalm 112 be on my life, and wealth and riches in my house. Thank You, Lord. I receive it and believe it, in Jesus's name.

Now let's pray together:

Heavenly Father,

Thank You for stability in my life. I will be a stable person. I will not be an unstable person. My heart is fixed and established. I will not have a double mind. I will not walk in double-mindedness and instability. I will not waver. I will be consistent in my giving and living.

Thank You, Lord, for giving me the grace and the power to be a godly, consistent, and righteous person. Lord, today I ask You to establish in my life anything that needs to be established. Fix in my life anything that needs to be fixed.

Thank You, Lord, for Your grace on my life. I receive wealth, prosperity, and blessing in my finances. Lord, thank You for Psalm 112. I receive it. I believe it. Let it be released in my life, in the name of Jesus. Amen.

DELIVERANCE CHECKUP

For all *have sinned and come short of the glory of God.*

—ROMANS 3:23, EMPHASIS ADDED

LL OF US have need of deliverance from time to time. There are no exceptions. As we grow in the Lord and in our discernment, we can begin to understand when we need spiritual victory in certain areas of our lives. Many times, as believers we can sense hindrances in our lives that keep us from living fully in the Spirit. Deliverance is an ongoing process in the life of a believer. It is a gift to us from God to keep us from being tormented by the enemy and living in our own cycles of bondage.

In their book *Pigs in the Parlor*, Frank and Ida Hammond named seven areas in our lives that will show signs that we need deliverance:[1]

1. Emotional problems
2. Mental problems
3. Speech problems
4. Sexual problems
5. Addictions
6. Physical infirmities
7. Religious error

When these problems begin to surface in our lives, we feel as if we are not successful. We may feel depressed, rejected, separated from God, and so on. This is what the enemy wants. But we have the help of the Holy Spirit, who can reveal to us the areas in which we need to be set free. We are also instructed to use our authority against the enemy and cast him out, ending his reign in our lives.

Below is a list you can use to evaluate yourself and your spiritual condition to see if you may need deliverance.

You May Need Deliverance If . . .

1. You were conceived in adultery or fornication. This can open the door for the spirit of lust.

2. Your parents contemplated an abortion. This can open the door for spirits of rejection, death, and fear.

3. You were given up for adoption. This can open the door for spirits of rejection, abandonment, and fear of abandonment.

4. You were abandoned by one or both parents. This can open the door for spirits of abandonment and fear of abandonment.

5. You were an orphan. This can open the door for spirits of rejection and abandonment.

6. You were abused as a child. This can open the door for spirits of rejection, fear, and hurt.

7. You were raped or molested. This can open the door for spirits of lust, shame, and hurt.

8. Your mother had a difficult pregnancy. This can open the door for spirits of fear that enter through trauma.

9. Your mother had a long and hard labor. This can open the door for spirits of fear that enter through trauma.

10. You almost died during your first few years of life. This can open the door for spirits of death and premature death.

11. You had imaginary playmates. This can open the door to spirits of rejection and loneliness.

12. You have been chronically ill all of your life. This can open the door to spirits of infirmity and death.

13. You have suffered from handicaps from childhood. This can open the door for spirits of rejection, shame, and fear.

14. You were exposed to pornography early in life. This can open the door to spirits of lust and perversion.

15. You saw something traumatic such as a murder or a fatal accident. This can open the door to spirits of fear and death.

16. You grew up in a war zone. This can open the door to spirits of fear and death.

17. You have been ridiculed all your life. This can open the door to spirits of rejection, fear of rejection, and self-rejection.

18. You ran away from home early in life. This can open the door to spirits of rejection and rebellion.

19. You have been chronically depressed. This can open the door to spirits of depression, rejection, sadness, and loneliness.

20. You have been diagnosed as manic depressive or schizophrenic. This can open the door to spirits of rejection, rebellion, and a root of bitterness.

21. You have had learning disabilities. This can open the door to spirits of rejection and fear.

22. You have been incarcerated. This can open the door to spirits of rejection, shame, and depression.

23. Your parent(s) were alcoholics. This can open the door to spirits of rejection and shame.

24. Your parents went through a divorce or separation. This can open the door to spirits of rejection and shame.

25. Your parents argued and fought in the home. This can open the door to spirits of confusion and fear.

26. You are angry or bitter with your parents, brothers, or sisters. This can open the door to spirits of anger and bitterness.

27. You were exposed to drugs at an early age. This can open the door to spirits of rebellion and witchcraft.

28. You are homosexual or lesbian, or were introduced to these lifestyles. This can open the door to spirits of lust and perversion.

29. You have a history of sexual perversion. This can open the door to spirits of lust and perversion.

30. You have been accident prone all your life. This is a sign of a curse.

31. You have a history of poverty in your or your family's life. This can be a manifestation of spirits of poverty and shame.

32. You have engaged in a lifestyle of cheating or theft. This can be a manifestation of spirits of lying and deceit.

33. You are or have been a chronic gambler or spend-thrift. This can be a manifestation of spirits of lust and addiction.

34. You are addicted to alcohol, drugs, nicotine, or food. This can be a manifestation of spirits of addiction and/or gluttony.

35. You are afraid of being alone. This can be a manifestation of spirits of fear.

36. You are afraid of leaving the house. This can be a manifestation of spirits of fear.

37. You are extremely uncomfortable around people. This can be a manifestation of spirits of rejection and fear.

38. You are intensely jealous of others. This can be a manifestation of spirits of jealousy and schizophrenia.

39. You hate certain groups of people (i.e., Jews, blacks, whites, Hispanics, and so on). This can be a manifestation of spirits of hatred and bigotry.

40. You were ever involved with the occult. This can open the door to spirits of witchcraft and the occult.

41. You have a history of freemasonry in your family. This can open the door to spirits of witchcraft and the occult.

42. You have attended a séance. This can open the door to spirits of witchcraft, sorcery, divination, and the occult.

43. You are attracted to or have gone to readers, advisers, and psychics. This opens the door to spirits of divination and witchcraft.

44. You were involved in the martial arts. This can open the door to spirits of mind control, witchcraft, and the occult.

45. You were involved in yoga or transcendental meditation. This can open the door to spirits of mind control and the occult.

46. You were involved in a false religion. This can open the door to spirits of religion, confusion, and deception.

47. You were involved in an abortion. This can open the door to spirits of murder and guilt.

48. You have gone through a divorce, separation, or a bad relationship. This can open the door to spirits of hurt, control, and rejection.

49. You have been controlled by your parents or any other person or group of people. This can open the door to spirits of mind control, fear, and control.

50. You have chronic headaches or mental confusion. This can be a manifestation of spirits of mind control and confusion.

51. You have a difficult time reading the Bible or praying. This can be a manifestation of Leviathan (spirit of pride).

52. You have a difficult time attending church. This can be a manifestation of Leviathan (spirit of pride).

53. You have a difficult time worshipping or praising God. This can be a manifestation of Leviathan (spirit of pride).

54. You hate being touched by people. This can be a manifestation of spirits of fear of giving and receiving love.

55. You are afraid of trusting people or getting close to people. This can be a manifestation of spirits of rejection and distrust.

56. You are a chronic liar. This can be a manifestation of spirits of lying and deception.

57. You are a chronic daydreamer. This can be a manifestation of the spirits of rejection and fantasy.

58. You are tormented by nightmares and bad dreams. This can be a manifestation of the spirits of fear and torment.

59. You have a problem with masturbation. This can be a manifestation of spirits of lust, masturbation, and perversion.

60. You dress provocatively or seductively. This can be a manifestation of spirits of lust and harlotry.

61. You wear too much jewelry or makeup. This can be a manifestation of spirits of rejection and self-rejection.

62. You have been tattooed or have multiple piercings. This can be a manifestation of spirits of rejection and rebellion.

63. You gossip, slander, and murmur constantly. This can be a manifestation of spirits of jealousy and rebellion.

64. You have attempted suicide or thought of killing yourself. This can be a manifestation of spirits of rejection, self-rejection, suicide, and rebellion.

65. You desire constant attention. This can be a manifestation of the spirit of rejection.

66. You constantly backslide and leave the church. This can be a manifestation of double-mindedness.

67. You go from church to church. This can be a manifestation of double-mindedness.

68. You have a problem letting go of the past. This can be a manifestation of unforgiveness and bitterness.

69. You are paranoid and think people are out to get you. This can be a manifestation of spirits of fear, distrust, and paranoia.

70. You are or have been a member of a legalistic church. This can open the door to spirits of religion, mind control, and witchcraft.

71. You had a controlling pastor or came from a controlling church or denomination. This opens the door to spirits of witchcraft, religion, and control.

72. You are still grieving of the death of a loved one although it has been years. This can open the door to a spirit of grief.

73. You constantly hear voices. This can be a manifestation of schizophrenia and paranoia.

74. You have a difficult time keeping a job, finding a job, or paying your bills. This can be a manifestation of spirits of poverty and vagabond.

75. You are always taken advantage of, abused, or misused by other people. This can open the door to spirits of rejection and abuse.

76. You have had miscarriages or are barren. This can open the door to spirits of infirmity and barrenness.

77. You are asthmatic, or have sinus problems or epilepsy. This can open the door to the spirit of infirmity.

78. You have psychic ability, can read people's minds, or know things not from the Lord. This can be a manifestation of psychic and occult spirits.

79. You were dedicated to the devil at an early age. This can open the door to spirits of witchcraft and death.

80. You have been rebellious or disobedient all of your life. This can be a manifestation of the spirits of rejection, rebellion, and/or double-mindedness.

81. You blame other people for all of your problems. This can be a manifestation of the spirit of accusation.

82. You can't rest or you have insomnia. This can be a manifestation of the spirits of insomnia, restlessness, and torment.

83. You are a perfectionist and become angry when things are not perfect. This can be a manifestation of the spirits of rejection, perfectionism, pride, and double-mindedness.

84. You are lazy, slothful, sloppy, and unorganized. This can be a manifestation of the spirits of rejection and double-mindedness.

85. You hate bathing and keeping yourself clean. This can be a manifestation of unclean spirits.

86. You are addicted to exercise and dieting. This can be a manifestation of spirits of rejection and self-rejection.

87. You are overly concerned about your appearance. This can be a manifestation of spirits of rejection, vanity, and self-rejection.

88. You feel ugly and unattractive. This can be a manifestation of spirits of rejection and self-rejection.

89. You are a workaholic and work yourself to exhaustion. This can be a manifestation of spirits of rejection and double-mindedness.

90. You are over-religious. This can be a manifestation of religious spirits and legalism.

91. You have a hard time believing God loves you. This can be a manifestation of spirits of rejection, self-rejection, doubt, and unbelief.

92. You are afraid of losing your salvation and going to hell. This can be a manifestation of the spirits of doubt, fear, religion, and legalism.

93. You are preoccupied with death and dying. This can be a manifestation of the spirit of death and fear.

94. You are a vagabond or wanderer. This can be a manifestation of the spirits of rejection and poverty.

95. You have a hard time submitting to authority. This can be a manifestation of spirits of rejection and rebellion.

96. You are unapproachable and hostile toward people. This can be a manifestation of the spirits of anger, hatred, rejection, and rebellion.

97. You are attracted to guns and weapons or keep them in your possession. This can be a manifestation of the spirits of rejection, rebellion, and double-mindedness.

98. You are afraid of demons, deliverance, and the subject of deliverance. This can be a manifestation of the spirit of fear.

99. You fall asleep in services and cannot pay attention. This can be a manifestation of Leviathan (the spirit of pride).

100. You have a preoccupation with religious symbols, clothing, icons, statues, etc. This can be a manifestation of religious spirits.

101. You have a preoccupation with horror movies and the macabre. This can be a manifestation of spirits of rejection, rebellion, and double-mindedness.

102. You have an inordinate affection for animals and pets. This can be a manifestation of double-mindedness.

103. You desire to drink blood or sacrifice animals. This can be a manifestation of spirits of witchcraft, occult, and rebellion.

104. You have ever murdered someone or have a desire to kill someone. This can be a manifestation of spirits of murder and death.

105. You have ever made pledges or oaths to false gods, Satan, occult, organizations, or gangs. This can be a manifestation of the spirits of the occult.

106. You have blasphemous thoughts constantly entering your mind, cursing God, etc. This can be a manifestation of blasphemy.

107. You are afraid of the police or authority figures. This can be a manifestation of the spirits of fear and fear of authority.

108. You are a loner and don't have any friends. This can be a manifestation of spirits of rejection and loneliness.

109. You have a desire to be naked and expose your body. This can be a sign of demonization.

110. You hate children or babies. This can be a manifestation of spirits of hatred and rejection.

Sometimes people would rather avoid deliverance. These people feel uncomfortable when you talk about demons, because they want to be left alone. Some people will give all kinds of excuses when it is time to pray in order to avoid the prayer of deliverance. Some will talk about their problems but resist when it comes time to pray.

People who need deliverance often withdraw from others and become isolated. The enemy will attempt to isolate them by keeping them away from the saints, fellowship, prayer, and deliverance services. Spirits of withdrawal and escapism are good at this and must be bound so that the person may be freed. Sometimes we feel that we have matured in the Lord to the point that we no longer need deliverance ministry.

When people don't want to be "bothered" or prayed for, and like being "left alone," it could be a tactic of the enemy to isolate them in order to keep them away from deliverance. But we should not respond this way. We should be humble as babes and remember that we go from glory to glory and faith to faith. It may be that when we are rising up to higher levels in God, new things are revealed to us, and new levels of deliverance are needed.

ADDITIONAL STRATEGIES FOR CASTING OUT THE ROOT OF BITTERNESS

Now no discipline seems to be joyful at the time, but grievous. Yet afterward it yields the peaceful fruit of righteousness in those who have been trained by it.

Therefore lift up your tired hands, and strengthen your weak knees. Make straight paths for your feet, lest that which is lame go out of joint, but rather be healed.

Pursue peace with all men, and the holiness without which no one will see the Lord, watching diligently so that no one falls short of the grace of God, lest any root of bitterness spring up to cause trouble, and many become defiled by it.

—HEBREWS 12:11–15, EMPHASIS ADDED

Notice in Hebrews 12:5 that the author starts out talking about the chastening of the Lord before he gets to the root of bitterness: "And you have forgotten the exhortation addressed to you as sons: 'My son, do not despise the discipline of the Lord, nor grow weary when you are rebuked by Him; for whom the Lord loves He disciplines.'"

God will discipline the heart of every true believer tempted with unforgiveness and bitterness to forgive that they may yield the "peaceful fruit of righteousness" (v. 11). A person has to forgive in order to break the power of bitterness.

When the chastening of the Lord is rejected, the root of bitterness springs up, troubling and defiling many (v. 15). We can clearly see the remedy given in Hebrews 12:11–13. We must be open to being trained by the discipline of the Lord.

Here are other spiritual tools that will help us see others or ourselves be set free from bitterness.

Blood of Jesus

> For you know that you were not redeemed from your vain way of life inherited from your fathers with perishable things, like silver or gold, but with the precious blood of Christ, as of a lamb without blemish and without spot.
> —1 Peter 1:18–19

The blood of Jesus is a true witness that delivers souls (Prov. 14:25; 1 John 5:8). Demons hate the blood of Jesus because it testifies and bears witness to the truth of our redemption. Satan is a false witness who speaks lies (Prov. 14:5, 25). The blood of Jesus has a voice and speaks of mercy (Heb. 12:24). The blood of Jesus reminds demons that our bodies belong to God (1 Cor. 6:20). Demons hate this because they regard the person's body as their house. Demons have no legal right to remain in a saint's body because of the blood of Jesus. We overcome Satan by the blood of the Lamb and the word of our testimonies (Rev. 12:11).

Communion

> The cup of blessing which we bless, is it not the communion of the blood of Christ? The bread which we break, is it not the communion of the body of Christ?
> —1 CORINTHIANS 10:16

Communion is the cup of blessing, the communion of the body and blood of Christ. Some spirits are driven out after the person receives prayer then "drinks of the blood of Christ" (spiritually speaking). This breaks their power and has proven to be powerful in destroying the strongholds of the enemy.

Break the spirit of bondage

> For you did not receive the spirit of bondage again to fear, but you received the Spirit of adoption by whom we cry out, "Abba, Father."
> —ROMANS 8:15, NKJV

Bondage means slavery. The spirit of bondage causes legalism, which promotes salvation by works instead of grace. This includes bondage to rules, regulations, and the traditions of men. The spirit of bondage causes fear of backsliding and fear of losing salvation.

- Bondage to man: Fear of man brings one into bondage (Prov. 29:25). "By whom a person is overcome, by him also he is brought into bondage" (2 Pet. 2:19, NKJV). Whether bondage to false teachers, prophets, or apostles (2 Cor. 11:13), soul ties need to be broken and spirits cast out (mind control, fear, deception, witchcraft).

- Bondage to organizations, lodges, cults, etc.: This type of bondage occurs through oaths, pledges, and vows to organizations or lodges such as Masons, Eastern Star, fraternities, sororities, cults, and clubs. Oaths bind the soul (Num. 30:2), and our souls need to be free to love the Lord (Matt. 22:37). These organizations have an effect on the soul even after one has left. Soul ties need to be broken and these organizations renounced.

- Bondage to self: We are told to deny ourselves (Mark 8:34). In order to be delivered from self, we must focus our attention on Jesus—"It is no longer I who live, but Christ who lives in me" (Gal. 2:20). This bondage to self manifests in selfishness and preoccupation with self. Spirits of self include self-awareness, self-love, self-condemnation, self-pity, self-consciousness, self-reward, self-deception, self-rejection, self-defense, self-torture, self-dependence, self-praise, self-destruction, selfishness, self-righteousness, and self-hatred.

NOTES

Chapter 1
Satan's Master Plan to Destroy the Human Race

1. Overview of *The Strange Case of Dr. Jekyll and Mr. Hyde*, Barnes and Noble http://www.barnesandnoble .com/w/dr-jekyll-and-mr-hyde-robert-louis-stevenson/100 0204307?ean=9781447820819 (accessed May 25, 2015).

2. Chuck D. Pierce and Robert Heidler, *A Time to Prosper* (Ventura, CA: Regal, 2013).

3. Pat Holliday, "Schizophrenia," DemonBuster.com www .demonbuster.com/schizophrenia.html (accessed May 25, 2015).

4. Frank and Ida Mae Hammond, *Pigs in the Parlor: A Practical Guide to Deliverance* (Kirkwood, MO: Impact Christian Books, 2010), 139.

5. Ibid., 140.

6. Albert Barnes, *Barnes' Notes on the Bible* (1834); Biblehub.com, http://biblehub.com/commentaries /barnes/james/1.htm (accessed May 25, 2015).

7. John Gill, *John Gill's Exposition of the Entire Bible* (1746–63); Biblehub.com, http://biblehub.com /commentaries/gill/james/1.htm (accessed May 25, 2015).

8. Dictionary.com, s.v. "excel," http://dictionary.reference .com/browse/excel (accessed May 26, 2015).

9. Robert Jamieson, A. R. Fausset, and David Brown, *A Commentary, Critical, Practical, and Explanatory on the Old and New Testaments* (Toledo, OH: Jerome B. Names & Co., 1886), Biblehub.com, http://biblehub.com /commentaries/jfb//psalms/119.htm (accessed May 25, 2015).

<h2 style="text-align:center">CHAPTER 2
UNSTABLE IN ALL THEIR WAYS</h2>

1. James Strong, *Strong's Exhaustive Concordance of the Bible*, s.v. "*dipsuchos*," http://biblehub.com/greek/1374 .htm (accessed May 27, 2015).

2. Bruce E. Levine, "How Teenage Rebellion Has Become a Mental Illness," AlterNet, http://www.alternet.org /story/75081/how_teenage_rebellion_has_become_a _mental_illness (accessed May 27, 2015).

3. Chris N. Simpson, "Freedom From the Deep Hurts of Rejection," NewWineMedia.com, http://www.newwine media.com/pastorchris/print/Chris_Simpson-Freedom _From_Deep_Hurts_Of_Rejection.pdf (accessed April 23, 2015).

4. List can be found at http://media.wix.com/ugd/2f18f4_6 d1aa88aeaa5afc409fcadf54bf3b7fc.pdf (accessed May 27,

2015). Every effort has been made to find the author of this material.

5. Chew Weng Chee, "The Absalom Spirit," September 25, 2011, Encouragement from the Word, http://tree-by -waters.blogspot.com/2011/09/absalom-spirit.html (accessed May 27, 2015).

6. Strong's Concordance, s.v. *"meshubah,"* http://biblehub .com/hebrew/4878.htm (accessed May 27, 2015).

7. Strong's Concordance, s.v. *"sarar,"* http://biblehub.com /hebrew/5637.htm (accessed May 27, 2015).

8. Strong's Concordance, s.v. *"shobab,"* http://biblehub.com /hebrew/7726.htm (accessed May 27, 2015); s.v. *"shub,"* http://biblehub.com/hebrew/7725.htm (accessed May 27, 2015); s.v. *"shobeb,"* http://biblehub.com/hebrew/7728 .htm (accessed May 27, 2015).

9. Strong's Concordance, s.v. *"maad,"* http://biblehub.com /hebrew/4571.htm (accessed May 27, 2015).

10. Strong's Concordance, s.v. *"stereóma,"* http://biblehub .com/greek/4733.htm (accessed May 27, 2015); s.v. *"ste- reoó,"* http://biblehub.com/greek/4732.htm (accessed May 27, 2015); s.v. *"stérigmos,"* http://biblehub.com/greek/4740 .htm (accessed May 27, 2015); s.v. *"stérizó,"* http:// biblehub.com/greek/4741.htm (accessed May 27, 2015).

Chapter 3
Stuck Between Two Opinions

1. John W. Ritenbaugh, "Knowing God: Bible Verses About Wavering," Forerunner Commentary, www.bibletools .org/index.cfm/fuseaction/Topical.show/RTD/cgg

/ID/1922/Wavering.htm#ixzz1Ocycmw2A (accessed
April 21, 2015).

2. Oxforddictionaries.com, s.v. "steadfast," http://www
.oxforddictionaries.com/us/definition/american_english
/steadfast (accessed May 27, 2015); Freedictionary.com,
s.v. "steadfast," http://www.thefreedictionary.com/stead
fast (accessed May 27, 2015).

3. Karl Lohman, "Groves," LearntheBible.com, http://www
.learnthebible.org/groves.html (accessed April 23, 2015);
Richard Ing, *Spiritual Warfare* (New Kensington, PA:
Whitaker House, 1996), 38–39, http://www.scribd.com
/doc/51810686/Spiritual-Warfare (accessed April 23,
2015).

4. Hammond, *Pigs in the Parlor.*

5. Ing, *Spiritual Warfare*, 49–50.

6. Bruce McConkie, *Doctrinal New Testament Commentary*, 3:248; see also The Church of Jesus Christ of
Latter-day Saints, "1 Kings 12–16: A Kingdom Divided
against Itself," Old Testament Student Manual Kings–
Malachi (1982), 41–50, https://www.lds.org/manual
/print/old-testament-student-manual-kings-malachi
/chapter-4.p1?lang=eng (accessed May 25, 2015).

7. The Church of Jesus Christ of Latter-day Saints, "1 Kings
12–16: A Kingdom Divided Against Itself," Old Testament Student Manual Kings–Malachi (1982), 41–50,
https://www.lds.org/manual/print/old-testament-student
-manual-kings-malachi/chapter-4.p1?lang=eng (accessed
May 25, 2015).

CHAPTER 4
THE DEVIL'S DOOR

1. Win Worley, *Rooting Out Rejection and Hidden Bitterness* (N.p.: WRW Publications LTD, 1991). Viewed online at http://21stcenturysaints.com/resources /Rooting-Out-Rejection-and-Hidden.pdf (accessed May 27, 2015).

2. Freedictionary.com, s.v. "megalomania," http://www.the freedictionary.com/megalomania (accessed May 27, 2015).

3. Noel and Phyl Gibson, *Excuse Me, Your Rejection Is Showing* (N.p.: Sovereign World Ltd., 2008); John Eckhardt, *God's Covenant with You for Deliverance and Freedom* (Lake Mary, FL: Charisma House, 2014), 30.

CHAPTER 5
AS THE SIN OF WITCHCRAFT

1. Derek Prince, *The Seeking of Control* www.scribd.com /doc/32202545/The-Seeking-of-Control-Rev-Derek -Prince (accessed April 29, 2014).

2. The Free Dictionary.com, s.v. "control," http://www.the freedictionary.com/control (accessed May 26, 2015).

3. Hissheep.org, "A Controlling Spirit—Poison in the Pot," www.hissheep.org/messages/a_controlling_spirit.html (accessed May 27, 2015).

4. Freedictionary.com, s.v. "possessive," http://www.thefree dictionary.com/possessive (accessed May 27, 2015).

5. Strong's Concordance, s.v. *"marah,"* http://biblehub.com /hebrew/4784.htm (accessed May 27, 2015).

CHAPTER 6
THAT WHICH DEFILES

1. Strong's Concordance, s.v. *"marah,"* http://biblehub.com /hebrew/4784.htm (accessed May 27, 2015).

2. Practical teachings and studies from the Word of God, "Root of Bitterness," GreatBibleStudy.com, http://www .greatbiblestudy.com/bitterness.php (accessed May 25, 2015).

3. David L. Cooper, "Rules of Interpretation: The Law of First Mention," *Biblical Research Monthly* 1947, 1949, http://www.biblicalresearch.info/page56.html (accessed May 25, 2015).

4. Blueletterbible.org, s.v. "Esau," http://www.blueletterbible .org/lang/lexicon/lexicon.cfm?strongs=H6215 (accessed July 2, 2015).

CHAPTER 7
FORGIVE AND BE HEALED

1. Spiritual roots of disease information has also been adapted from Life Application Ministries, "Are Some Diseases a Spiritual Condition?", http://www.life applicationministries.org/root.htm (accessed May 25, 2015); Henry Wright, "Spiritually Rooted Diseases," Free Republic, January 19, 2010, http://www.freerepublic.com /focus/f-religion/2432288/posts (accessed May 25, 2015).

2. Wright, "Spiritually Rooted Diseases."

3. A great source that shows the connection between emotional and psychological issues and autoimmune disease is an article by Gail Berger, "Autoimmune Disease &

Histories of Stress," http://www.nature-nurture.org /index.php/chronic-stress/chronic-stress-human /histories-autoimmune/ (accessed May 25, 2015).

4. Medline Plus, "Autoimmune Disorders," July 16, 2013, http://www.nlm.nih.gov/medlineplus/ency/article/000816 .htm (accessed May 25, 2015).

5. Wright, "Spiritually Rooted Diseases."

6. Ibid.

7. WebMD, "Diabetes Overview," http://www.webmd.com /diabetes/diabetes-overview (accessed May 25, 2015).

8. PubMed Health, "Psychological and Social Issues: Emotional and Behavioural Problems," 2004, http://www.ncbi .nlm.nih.gov/pubmedhealth/PMH0015995/ (accessed May 27, 2015).

9. Wright, "Spiritually Rooted Diseases."

10. Ibid.

11. The Body of Christ Deliverance Ministry, "The Roots of Disease: General Overview," http://www.thebocdm.com /the-roots-of-disease.html (accessed May 25, 2015).

12. Ibid.

13. Wright, "Spiritually Rooted Diseases."

14. Ibid.

15. Strong's Concordance, s.v. "*Marah*," http://biblehub.com /hebrew/4785.htm (accessed May 25, 2015).

16. Strong's Concordance, s.v. "*marah*," http://biblehub.com /hebrew/4784.htm (accessed May 25, 2015).

CHAPTER 8
DIVIDE AND CONQUER

1. Gene Moody, *Deliverance Manual* (Baton Rouge, LA: Deliverance Ministries), digital version, http://www.gene moody.com/assets/001-moody-deliverance-manual-p.i -p60.pdf (accessed May 27, 2015).

2. Frank Hammond, "Schizophrenia," LHBCOnline. com, http://lhbconline.com/frank-ida-mae-hammond/ (accessed July 2, 2015).

3. Gene and Earline Moody, "Deliverance Manual: Schizo-phrenia," DemonBuster.com, http://www.demonbuster .com/schizop3.html (accessed May 26, 2015).

4. Frank and Ida Mae Hammond, *Pigs in the Parlor* (Kirk-wood, MO: Impact Christian Books, 1973).

5. *Merriam-Webster's Collegiate Dictionary*, 11th Edition (Springfield, MA: Merriam-Webster Incorporated, 2003), s.v. "bind."

6. Merriam-Webster Online, s.v. "trauma," http://www .merriam-webster.com/dictionary/trauma (accessed May 27, 2015).

7. Strong's Concordance, s.v. *"pharmakeia,"* http://biblehub .com/greek/5331.htm (accessed May 27, 2015).

CHAPTER 10
BECOME A PSALM 112 BELIEVER

1. Freedictionary.com, s.v. "single-minded," http://www .thefreedictionary.com/single-minded (accessed May 27, 2015).

2. Blueletterbible.org, s.v. *"haplous,"* http://www.blueletter bible.org/lang/lexicon/lexicon.cfm?Strongs=G573&t=KJV (accessed May 27, 2015).

Appendix A
Deliverance Checkup

1. Hammond, *Pigs in the Parlor*.

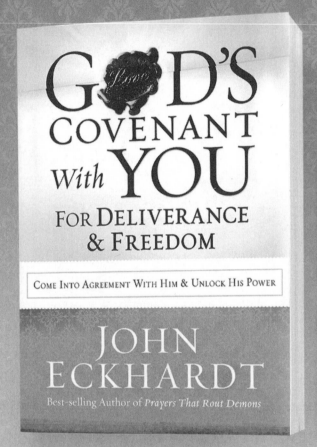

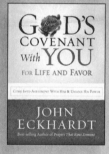